# PRAISE FOR SPEAK THE UN

In her new book, *Speak the Unspeakable*, Elizabeth Good has cut the human experience open and helped us to see ourselves through a lens that is both hopeful and extremely honest about what is wrong and how to have some self- and spiritual intelligence on going after making it right. It's a completely unique read that would help any spiritual maturity level grow into a new version of ourselves. It spends just the right amount of presenting a case and research for how we are wired to confess, to open up, to process. But Elizabeth also shares very touching and real stories both from her personal life and from people she is around. The book reminds me of the Message version of the Bible in Matthew 5:8: "You're blessed when you get your inside world—your mind and heart—put right. Then you can see God in the outside world." I think this book helps us to do just that.

**Shawn Bolz**
**TV Host, Commentator**
**Journalist, Podcaster, Author, Minister**

In a world where secrets, masks, and highlight reels are rampant, Elizabeth Good shines a bold and beautiful invitation to *Speak the Unspeakable*. When I first learned that Elizabeth helps people, especially pastors, come out of secrecy about porn addiction, sexual abuse, and more—she became an instant hero of mine. I pray this important book and movement spreads like wildfire so that our churches and society can reignite with truth, restoration, and authentic community.

**Rachel Thomas, Sex Trafficking Survivor-Leader**
**Executive Director of Ending the Game and**
**Member of the White House Advisory Council**

Elizabeth Good's message through *Speak the Unspeakable* is crucial for the world. Leaders can no longer stay silent when it comes to gender inequality, sexual violence and exploitation, and generational abuses. We must take courage, raise our voice, and take action to bring these things to light. This book and Elizabeth's work around the world give us hope that change in our personal lives, faith communities, and governments is vital and achievable.

**Rozalia Biro**
**Member of the Romanian Parliament and President/**
**Chair of the Committee on Foreign Affairs**

Everyone has secrets. Some burn down your soul! This book is a tell-all for how to PUT OUT THE FIRE!

**Lynne Jubilee Cumming, Chair, The Foundation United**

*Speak the Unspeakable* carries a treasured, unique, anointed, and urgent message of hope for our churches, our families, our children, and for us. First, we see that we cannot walk in our calling when we are trapped in our past. Then, we go on to see how churches, families, and parents can change to become havens of hope; instead of walking alone with our secrets, we become free to speak and pray about our fears, traumas, and abuses. And she gives us fresh new language for talking with our children and grandchildren about accessing help when they face such matters. We are blessed by using the "keys" Elizabeth shares, reminding us "to ask for where the good way is, and walk in it, and find rest for our souls" (Jeremiah 6:16). These keys unlock transformational healing, so that we live walking in full freedom—together, not alone—to fulfill our calling and purpose in Christ Jesus our Lord.

**Dr. Susan Hillis, Global Coordinator for Strategy,**
*World Without Orphans*

Elizabeth Good is an exceptional, beautiful, and talented person who could go far in the secular world of today, but she has chosen to devote her life to helping those who have been abused and need love and care. Her book *Speak the Unspeakable* is a rich combination of her own experiences and her advice to those who are seeking help. She approaches the material from her own experiences together with much expertise gained from working with others. The book is a must read for those who desire inward help after being abused and those who desire to help others.

**Professor William Wagner**
**President Emeritus Olivet University**
**Founder of Global Strategy Forum**
**Advisor to the World Evangelical Association**

Elizabeth Melendez Good deserves our prayers, support, and encouragement for the fearless crusade she and many others are on to shine a light on sexual sin within the church and in the process help many men and women of faith to become free from the bondage of sexual sin. Through confidential discussions that I have had with Christian men in African churches, I am convinced that the challenge of sexual sin is not just an American or European problem but a GLOBAL problem. I applaud Elizabeth for having the courage to speak the unspeakable, the faith to believe that the same Jesus Christ who saved her from sin will equip her for the journey of blessing others through this ministry, and the perseverance to write this book that will shine a light into dark places. Congratulations, Elizabeth! May God bless you and bless REAL TALK.

**Modupe S. Taylor-Pearce, PhD., Freetown, Sierra Leone**

"What we hear in the darkness, proclaim from the rooftops." Secrecy is Satan's best tool. *Speak the Unspeakable* brings out of the shadows the dark reality of abuse and trafficking. This book will give the courage and the tools that lead to justice and recovery.                                    **Fr. M. Jeffery Bayhi**

The deepest part of the human heart longs for freedom to be everything we were created and redeemed to be. Yet the traumas of life and evil unseen forces are at work keeping us from living out our purpose. In a culture where people are striving to be heard but don't have words or processes for their pain, Elizabeth Good is being used by God as a voice and champion of freedom. Her honest, bold, and heartfelt passion for people to be free clearly permeates through the pages of this book. The authenticity and vulnerability in which she shares her own story moves you to take action and follow the outlined steps in this book for your own personal freedom. As a man who has experienced the shame and pain of being abused, and the freedom that has come through the excavation process of God's love, I believe that this book, *Speak the Unspeakable*, and the course, Real Talk, will be a catalyst that will launch a generation into their healing and destiny. Thank you, Elizabeth, for writing this powerful, insightful, challenging, and motivating book.
**Pastor Burnard Scott Jr., Bayside Community Church**

Real Talk, real life, real relationships. As a pastor, my heart breaks for leaders who do not have the freedom to experience those three things. God's Word tells us to confess our sins to one another, yet few Christians are actively following this truth. As believers, we are given the ministry of reconciliation. True reconciliation comes as we follow the truth of confessing our sins to one another. In this book, Elizabeth is giving us the tools to walk in full freedom to be a transparent light on a hill. In my life and in the lives of people in our congregation, I have witnessed the transforming power of God as our secrets were shared. The victories have been nothing short of miraculous.
**Danny Allen, Senior Pastor, Blue Ridge Community Church**

Poignant and powerful, Elizabeth invites the reader to a deeply personal level of vulnerability by articulating a clear path to life-changing freedom. She provides the keys to getting unstuck and pulling out roots of brokenness. She exposes the enemy's tactics and how the church has unknowingly fallen for them. This is a fresh revolutionary approach to empowering people to reclaim their identity and value. It is a must read for all churches and leaders.
**Mallory Bashom, Gateway Network Pastor**

*Speak the Unspeakable* unlocks the truth that is vital for every church and is a vital read for leaders and parents. REAL TALK is the missing link for believers. I have been in ministry for over 30 years and have led every area from children and youth to young adults, seniors, and everyone in between... I have seen again and again that life-controlling secrets and shame often stand between them and freedom. We must have these hard conversations and offer a way for our congregations to heal and process. As a survivor of childhood sexual abuse, I love Elizabeth's heart to help children be protected from this evil and help adults have tools to be free from their past experiences. We haven't had a tool like this before, and we are excited to embrace REAL TALK in our church. **Nancy Turpin, Pastor, Westcoast Church**

*Speak the Unspeakable* is a must read for anyone who has fallen prey to a predator or who wants to support someone who has. Step by step, Elizabeth Good teaches survivors how to break through shame, secrecy, and silence to reclaim their truest selves, reminding us all how to live the life we were born to live.
**Julie Cantrell**
*New York Times* **and USA Today**
**bestselling author of** *The Feathered Bone*

As someone who was told that exposing darkness and abuse in the church would damage the cause of Christ, I appreciate Elizabeth's call for transparency and healing through confession. When secrets are brought to the light, there is freedom and healing, which is missing in the church today. It is time.
**Naghmeh Abedini Panahi**
**Author of** *I Didn't Survive: Emerging Whole After Deception*
*Persecution, And Hidden Abuse*

In *Speak the Unspeakable*, Elizabeth Fisher Good starts by asking readers if there is more to life than what they are currently experiencing. With that simple question, she is off to the races with wisdom and tools gleaned from personal experience and decades of ministering to those aching to live out their God-designed purpose. This book will help you find that purpose as well. **Debbie Kraulidis, Vice President, Moms For America**

Bravo, Elizabeth Good, for having the courage to "speak the unspeakable" and open the door to true freedom for people all over the world. With a powerful mixture of vulnerability, humility, and passion, Good shares her story of overcoming the destructive effects of abuse, addiction, and shame through what she calls "the lost art of confession" and stepping into the "more" that God has for her. She invites readers into the same difficult, redemptive, and transformative process and outlines a new curriculum called Real Talk that helps individuals, churches, ministries, and businesses dare to *Speak the Unspeakable* and move toward the wholeness and freedom God has intended for His children.

**Elizabeth Musser**
**Author of *By Way of the Moonlight***
***The Swan House*, and *The Promised Land***

Working as a doctor for thirty years in suburban private practice, in hospitals, and now with clinics in the world's slums has taught me one thing—everyone has a story. Whether we're ready to talk about it or not, there are pains that run deep. We cover them up in public, but they are wounds that are killing us and killing our children. We don't have safe spaces to speak about the unspeakable. My friend Elizabeth has her own story, a story that she learned to hide as a child, a story that no one else knew. As a glamorous and successful career woman, she hid the pain and shame well, but that story was killing her and those she loved most. Then someone gave her the most unlikely safe space to begin speaking about her own unspeakable story, and she began the journey of becoming truly alive from the inside out. Elizabeth's story gives us hope for our own story and for the stories of those around us. She shows us the power of creating a safe place for ourselves and others to speak about the unspeakable and reminds us that we weren't made to carry these pains alone. There is hope for us, for our kids, and for generations to come.

**Stephen Letchford, MD, President, Banda Health**

The book is fabulous and life-changing. It has given me the courage to speak dark unspeakable things and find healing not only for myself, but for those I get to work with on a daily basis. Elizabeth teaches us that Real Talk is desperately needed in our families, churches, workplaces, and anywhere you have a relationship. You will not be the same after reading this book. It will give you hope and encouragement to go *Speak the Unspeakable* and bring healing to your part of the world.

**Staci Yates, My House**
**Director of Human Trafficking Recovery Services, Alaska Stop**
**Human Trafficking Chair, Alaska's Governor Council on Human and**
**Sex Trafficking, and survivor of sex trafficking**

Bravo! Elizabeth, you put your finger in the wound, the wound of the church. It is painful, but somebody needed to point to this wound because we need help. This book does not judge; rather, you invite people into a life without secrets. You invite people into a life of liberty, freedom, and shalom...and it all begins with "speaking the unspeakable." The book does not give all the answers but invites us on a beautiful journey. You give examples of how you have changed and inspire others to want to do the same. It is a challenging read that leads to new thoughts, and that, in my opinion, is the best. Timely and greatly needed.

**Alex Berg, Pastor**
**Mosaik-Kirche wie eine Familie, Erftstadt, Germany**

Elizabeth Good is the perfect voice to accelerate the discussion that we need to be having right now! She applies a delicate balance of gentleness and boldness as she addresses a very challenging topic. Additionally, she does a wonderful job of helping the reader navigate into these difficult areas with a comforting reminder of the promise of hope and healing in God's sovereignty and power. This is a MUST read!

**Joe Pringle, President National Christian Foundation-Chicago**

This book is a message with several layers. The devastation of sexual abuse in childhood is known, and often hidden, deep in the hearts of many adults. However, the hiding does not stop, or even control, the devastation of this unspeakable secret. Some mental health professionals doubt that devastation can ever be stopped. This author believes it can and offers a strategy to win the battle. Elizabeth reveals the power of words to destroy the destroyer. She encourages the victims to speak the secrets in confession, embrace a new and wonderful purpose, fight the battle, grab the victory, and hold on to a new and better life. In addition, she provides step-by-step instructions on how to win this war. *Speak the Unspeakable* relies on the Word of God, trusts His power, and expects final victory. This book is desperately needed today. It will help many hurting people escape the prison of early, or recent, abuse and gain a good life that will change everything.

**Rev. Dr. Terry Raburn, Superintendent**
**Peninsular Florida District Council of the Assemblies of God**
**Chair of the Board of Trustees, Southeastern University**

There often comes a time when the Lord shines a brighter light on an area He wants the body of Christ to focus on. Beginning with her book *Groomed* and now with *Speak the Unspeakable*, Elizabeth Good has drawn back a large curtain behind which those who have been sexually abused and trafficked have hidden but are now invited to come to the light of Jesus. By "speaking the unspeakable" of their past to trusted, trained confidants, they can experience forgiveness with deep healing, then join the rapidly growing numbers in the fight to confront this growing evil that is especially directed toward vulnerable children globally. After a chapter or two, you will not want to put this book down!

**Allan H. Beeber, Ph.D., MBA**
**Senior Cru Connector: Collaborations and Partnerships**

# ELIZABETH GOOD

# SPEAK

## THE

# UNSPEAKABLE

### REAL TALK
#### ON SECRETS, SEX, AND
### BEING SET FREE

WHITAKER
HOUSE

*Speak the Unspeakable* is based on the author's personal experiences and research. It is intended for informational purposes only, not to replace or supersede consulting with a licensed, practicing medical or healthcare professional. The publisher and author are not responsible for any residual or resulting effects from acting on the concepts presented in this book. Every reasonable effort has been made to ensure accuracy and value. Always seek the advice of your own medical or mental health provider regarding any questions or concerns you have about your specific circumstances.

**Speak the Unspeakable:** Real Talk on Secrets, Sex, and Being Set Free

ISBN: 979-8-88769-047-6
eBook ISBN: 979-8-88769-048-3

Printed in the United States of America

© 2023 by Elizabeth Good

Whitaker House
1030 Hunt Valley Circle
New Kensington, PA 15068
www.whitakerhouse.com

Library of Congress Control Number: 2023942031

1 2 3 4 5 6 7 8 9 10 11 ᴟ 30 29 28 27 26 25 24 23

# DEDICATION

To my precious "Up Line" and "Down Lines." Mom and Dad, my "Up Line," this last year has been the greatest gift. Thank you for the privilege of walking with you through the many doors that have previously been locked. What a gift to pray through your secrets and hear your stories! And to my dynamic "Down Line," Sammi, Max, and Leo, I am so thankful that you all love each other and love God, my most heartfelt prayer since you all were born! You are now the authors of the narrative; the generational secrets are on the table. I know you will live forward well in powerful generational freedom! I love you all so much!

And to Mr. Good, thank you for stepping into this wild ride of a narrative! I love you tremendously!

# TABLE OF CONTENTS

## PART 4: RELEASE

## PART 5: RELAUNCH

# A JOURNEY TO LIVING BOLDLY AUTHENTIC, BRAVELY TRANSPARENT, AND UNAPOLOGETICALLY FREE

"No risk it, no biscuit."
—NFL Coach Bruce Arians

The moment God thought of you, creation met purpose. The moment you were knit together, you were knit to a purpose. It's a perfect plan. But in an imperfect world, when person meets purpose is also the minute the battle begins. Thankfully, you were born to battle.

The enemy wants to separate us from our purpose by any means, and he knows how to speak the language of your weaknesses—whatever fear, anxiety, rejection, or story from your past is plaguing you and holding you back. Your purpose is not dependent on an "if." It's a biblical promise that there's something amazing you're called to do. Stepping into that divine, eternal purpose requires a deep-down excavation that's worth the risk.

The process might require facing things you find unspeakable, speaking up about things you've left unspoken, or being the catalyst of total culture change—whether in your own life, home, and family, or creating systemic change around you in your community, your church, or on a global scale.

That may sound ambitious, but nothing is impossible when it comes to how God can use a single life when you are totally surrendered, totally free from the unhealthy voices of your past or present, and totally aligned with where He is calling you to go.

That calling is why we're here—on the pages of this book and in the world. You exist for an eternal reason, and not being active in that reason can lead to a sense of unrest, disconnection, frustration, and unfulfillment. Chances are you know that; you feel that you were meant for more, but you don't know how to get there. I understand all too well. It's where I was. Where I began. But it's not where I stayed. If you're ready, you won't stay there either.

***

We're trained to keep our secrets…secret. In some cases, we're culturally *Groomed* (as described in my last book)[1] that letting our secrets out will devastate us and everyone around us. In reality, keeping them hidden does the most damage. We have to fully excavate and properly process anything and everything that holds us back, so it doesn't have power over our "now" or our future.

That's where I was—living the "perfect" life on paper, but unable to quiet the rising voice within me saying I was made for more and that God didn't want me settling for less. Because of what the Bible promises, I believe there is a hand-in-glove fit with God's purposes for which every person is intentionally created.

With all I'd accomplished, learned, and led, I really wasn't even looking to pivot and didn't even know if it was possible, or if I was just

---

1. Elizabeth Melendez Fisher Good, *Groomed: Overcoming the Messages That Shaped Our Past and Limit Our Future* (Nashville: Thomas Nelson, 2020).

crazy and selfish for wanting more. Aiming for it and asking God to show me how has led to a greater calling than I'd ever known. I'm convinced this is a biblical promise, which means the same opportunity is available to absolutely every person. Including you.

***

For three decades I learned through observing the world in extremes:

**Round One:** In corporate America, working in marketing and media in Chicago, there weren't many secrets. As you can imagine, secular urban culture lets it all hang out; hardly anything is unspoken or hidden. On the contrary, what would normally be kept under the table is flaunted, celebrated, and high-fived. There's openness, but without God's guidance for how to use that transparency for good, it only makes things worse.

**Round Two:** From one extreme to the other, I served for almost a decade as a leader and area pastor at Willow Creek Community Church. In a ministry of that size and global reputation, you're steeped in biblical principles, but as is so often the case in church culture (especially in large ministries where you don't want to get too close to the wheels of the machine), you just pick a little off the top that you can handle, and if there are bigger, deeper, more troubling issues, you don't really "go there." It's too risky or too hard to fly it up the flagpole. You keep it unspoken—until everything implodes and everyone asks, "Why didn't someone say something sooner?"

**Round Three:** When I moved into the nonprofit sector, I started to see the first hints of the secret sauce that had the potential to bring a powerful, purpose-launching openness up and out of everyone. Working with women involved in sex trafficking, we used to hand out these cards that had information on one side to help them realize they were "made for more." The back of this card said simply, "Ever Wonder if There Is More? Are You Ready?" As I began to see women's reactions to this invitation—from those who had never heard that hope before to those who had been trying to silence it in their heart for years—I realized this message isn't just for people in obvious, trials-based lifestyles of tragedy and trauma. It's for every single one of us.

When I combined this long-term path of development that I was on and put the shared experiences of these different environments together, *I began to see the recipe for what's missing from the world in every setting:*

The bold and brash **secular business world** or "marketplace" talks openly, easily, and hides little, but it lacks the biblical tools and compassion to leverage that transparency.

**Church ministry** focuses directly on those biblical tools but applies them strictly on the surface of "acceptable" issues. It stays safely on the surface, distancing itself from so many deeper issues—all too often resulting in denial in the form of a cover-up culture, which makes it easy to veer into deception and, God forbid, scandal.

The hard but hopeful hearts trapped in the **sex trafficking** industry bury both the Bible and the boldness to speak up and to "name your pimp," literally or figuratively, regarding the abusive voices that led them where they were, eliminating the ability to push back against the groomers and influencers responsible for the "messages that shaped our past and limit our future."[2] This is the epitome of having no armor, no tools, no leverage for change.

If the right formula doesn't exist in these spaces—transparency, confession, healing, listening, and service—where does it exist? The answer should be, and was originally intended to be, the church. The truth is, in our contemporary society, it doesn't exist—anywhere.

What's the secret to creating a transformational, healing space that doesn't fully exist anywhere else? The key ingredient is facing the very thing you think you can't say, admit, confront, or handle, and giving it enough air to let it wither and die out. Disarm the seemingly

---

2. Good, *Groomed.*

impenetrable web of lies Satan spends all his time weaving by turning the light on what's been hidden and realizing it can't kill you. Name your pimp, the voices that held or hold you back, and watch them lose their power.

The deeper answer for *how* to walk through those steps and to do so in a lasting manner you can carry with you into a life of new habits, breaking cycles, changing direction, and influencing generations, is a program being implemented everywhere from local classrooms to international parliaments:

> *REAL TALK:*
> *A TOOL CREATED TO HELP YOU OPEN UP,*
> *SPEAK UP, AND RISE UP,*
> *TO PLACE GOD AND TRUTH AT THE CENTER*
> *OF THE CONVERSATION.*

People who are discovering how to "speak up and live free" are saying by the thousands, "This changes everything." What we're about to embark on in this book unpacks the "this" that "changes everything" page by page, with the support of the program behind it and the team that's already committed to your success and spiritual healing. We don't know you yet. But we do know a lot about what you've been through, because we've been there. And now we work every day with new "been there" stories, and we're always learning and developing ever more tools to help you *Speak the Unspeakable* and live unspeakably free.

*** 

There's more, though, and this might be the most important part:

# TIME IS OF THE ESSENCE.

This isn't a devotional or your standard spiritual growth exercise. This is an alarm. A bullhorn. An urgent outcry. Time is so vital for each individual standing in front of their purpose, for every person around you, and for every unfolding generation affected by what you choose to do—what others watch you choose, right now.

Our kids and those we influence are our greatest audience. They have a front-row seat to the choices we make and the habits we form. If we're polishing our imperfections, concealing our conflicts, disguising our demons, feeling like we must look perfect on the outside while barely getting by on the inside, then we're dying on the vine and perpetuating self-destruction in others.

"Fake it till you make it" will never move you into "make it" territory. We just get stuck faking it until our secrets die with us. Worse, we condemn countless others to a death sentence of repeating the cycle.

The alternative choice is that you can be the big bad boulder in the stream that redirects a powerful flow of water. You can decide, simple as that, to break the cycle and let your "real" happen.

God has provided you all the keys you need to open (or shut!) any door you come up against. We're about to learn how to recognize the doors, face them, and turn the key. Depending on the door, these keys can be used to open a barrier that's blocking your progress, or lock forever a seemingly inescapable avenue of pain and shame and "stay in your healing," which is a conversation we'll get into in chapter 10, "No Going Back."

You should know, this isn't for the faint of heart. Though it's true that everyone is "Born to Battle" (chapter 7), not everyone feels ready. For those who are, *Speak the Unspeakable* (and the ongoing work in the

Real Talk program) walks you through the "messages and mindsets that hold you back from your God-given identity" to "unleash your full eternal purpose and legacy."[3]

When you accept that you were "Made for More" (chapter 2) and do the work of "Embracing Your Eternal Purpose" (chapter 9), you start to believe you deserve "The Good Life" (chapter 11) and realize it's not just for or about you—on the contrary, "This Changes Everything" (chapter 12).

People are starving for truth, and it's not the lead story anywhere. That's *my* eternal purpose—I feel like I have an antidote, and I can't stay quiet about it. *We need to talk.* It's time. For me, my family, and the real people and organizations involved in the Real Talk movement, we're finally embracing our eternal purpose and living the Good Life God designed for us from the moment He devised our purpose. Through the pages of this book, I invite you to do the same.

---

3. Free With E: Organizational Mission Statement.

# PART 1:

# RECEIVE

# CHAPTER 1

# WE NEED TO TALK

"I've never told anyone this before..."

I said that myself.

"I've never told anyone this before."

When I finally did "tell all"—when I opened up and learned how to *Speak the Unspeakable*—everything changed, for Good.

So, I said it more than once, about more than one secret I had been carrying around for my entire life. These secrets weren't small, like cheating on a math test or slipping a lipstick into my purse without paying for it. They involved my marriage, my family; childhood sexual abuse, peer-on-peer abuse, and rape; numbing and repeating learned behaviors; pornography, abortion; open doors to the occult and idolatry in many ways—all of which had combined to produce a paralyzing shame. And that's only a partial list.

I used to hide everything, not only out of shame but in a very successful attempt at pretending to be perfect. I don't hide anything anymore.

That ship has long since sailed. By now I've told the world everything—in TED talks, conferences, and my previous book *Groomed*, where I first exposed my most damaging experiences in painstaking detail in writing. I don't regret it. I haven't stopped. Lord willing, I never will.

I share these stories every chance I get, from internationally influential platforms to quiet rooms where a single life is on the verge of waking up and walking differently. Every time I do, I hear someone say the words that changed my life and are about to change theirs: *"I've never told anyone this before..."*

I hear it from leaders, celebrities, kids. I hear it from the trafficked and prominent families. I hear it almost without exception from every walk of life. So, if you're thinking right now that there's something you haven't said, faced, or disarmed from your past, you can know immediately, you're not alone.

You also might want to steady yourself, because I haven't seen anyone come across these keys and keep going unaffected, unchallenged, or unchanged. It's foundation-shifting, sometimes whether we like it or not, and the process isn't always easy. No matter the ease or level or difficulty, I also haven't seen anyone go through this process and not whisper or shout from their elevated vantage point: "It's worth it."

## SPEAKING THE UNSPEAKABLE

Research shows that being heard registers in the brain as feeling loved.[4] I get to see this day after day as people respond to being heard, accepted, and given the tools to process what needs to be repurposed in their lives in order for them to move forward.

As I shared in *Groomed*, one in three women reports being sexually abused as a child—91 percent of those by people the victim knew.[5] Sixty percent of adults report experiencing abuse or other difficult family

---

4. Carl Nassar, *The Importance of Feeling Understood.*
5. http://victimsofcrime.org/media/reporting-on-child-sexual-abuse/child-sexual-abuse-statistics

circumstances during childhood.[6] These scars carry into adulthood. An abused person is more likely to enter an abusive relationship and pass it on to their children, who will probably repeat the cycle, if not escalate it.

Grief, shame, and fear, when they are not fully processed, keep replaying and write a repetitive script of unfulfilled, broken messaging from which our lives never deviate. The pattern is evident not only in our lives; staying in our brokenness negatively affects the lives of those we influence, our loved ones, or, God forbid, new victims with whom we live out the effects of our personal traumas.

## WE DON'T JUST LIVE BROKEN, WE "BREAK IT FORWARD."

About sexual abuse specifically (the most prominent and shame-oriented among life's secrets), you may have heard the "one in three girls and one in five boys"[7] statistic before, and if you have, it's sometimes easy to gloss over. We become numb to the numbers. But stop for a moment and think about what that means: roughly a third of our entire population. On average, one out of every five people *who you know* carry this secret.

Now "break it forward" from there: Consider that abused individuals almost always enact this behavior in some form toward another child or in an adult relationship. That means a new third of the population is being abused by a victim of abuse. These numbers aren't just from or for an "out of sight, out of mind" mission field like sex trafficking, where many are working to reach a more "obviously" hurting world. It's where you'd least imagine. It's in our neighborhoods and schools. It's on the

---

6. http://justice.aksummit.com/PDF/081712_childhood_trauma.pdf
7. Carol Shakeshaft, Congressional Report; Hofstra University School of Education

PTA and in the classroom. It's in our church. It's in our family. Turn and look to your left and then to your right; if not you, it's them.

## IT STARTS WITH ME...TOO

When I share my own secrets, which I've now come to own and feel the power of sharing, I see in others when the lightbulb goes on. They've been in the dark so long, and when they realize they can get free of their secrets and get in touch with purpose, they start to breathe in hope and reinflate. It gives them permission to dream.

My life—including all of these stories about my past—is on the table for anyone to see. Traumatic accidental deaths in my family; abortion; sexual abuse from more than one source from childhood through my teenage years; a previous marriage plagued by pornography and emotional/verbal abuse. When I share openly about the sexual abuse that I endured from a trusted family friend and platform church leader, hands in the room shoot up from people who have long been desperate to share and find release and relief from their pain. Their openness is a reflection of my own. My brutal, total transparency about everything encourages others to share their own stories... and wow, do they share.

There are different layers of **degradation** tied to different layers of **declaration**. There are things we're more accustomed to hearing (abuse within the family, or from teachers or babysitters) where people are a little less surprised and a little more likely to say, "Me too." Then you get into deeper excavations and more turbulent shock waves. "I was abused by my pastor." "A prominent community leader has been sleeping with their direct reports for their whole career—and their staff knows about it." "I was trafficked by adults who involved me in child pornography." "I've participated in the sex industry by buying girls." "After I was abused, I abused others." These things are harder to say.

No matter how many times you level up, how unheard of the story seems, I can guarantee you, someone out there needs to hear you tell your story so that while you're gaining freedom from it, they can say, "Me too."

One of the areas this crops up the most is with men, who think sexual abuse "just doesn't happen to men." Through my decade of bringing light into the darkness of sex trafficking, it's true that the stories we faced involved a staggering 85 percent of women and girls versus one in five or 20 percent of men and boys. Because of this vast majority, many assume this is not a common issue for men—but it's not nearly exclusive to women.

We've found through Real Talk conversations that men are just as likely to be carrying the weight of shame, perhaps more as they're even less likely to speak up about something that's happened to them, thinking they *really are* the only one. That couldn't be further from the truth, and when one man has the brawn to tell his story, he tees it up for another.

One Real Talk participant stepped forward to unburden that he lived his entire life with a mortifying, paralyzing embarrassment that irreparably damaged his relationship with his father, who walked in on him being abused by another boy but mistakenly thought it was consensual. Because this man was never given the tools to speak up and explain what he was being put through, he paid a price for the rest of his life. He and his father never spoke of it again, and he carried that shame. Until he heard someone tell a similar story and realized he could finally step out of the past, he never dreamed there was a way for him to recover and live an entirely, eternally different future.

(Throughout this book, you'll run into a million concepts that you'll want to share with those who might need to hear them. One of the most valuable concepts to pass on is this one about the commonality of men affected by abuse, because it's one that most are least likely to have heard and might be shocked and relieved to discover. And let's not leave out addiction, for both men and women.)

## NONDISCLOSURE "AGREEMENT"

Several celebrity cases of abuse that have hit the headlines over the past few decades can be traced back to unconfessed and unprocessed childhood abuse that set the table for that person to grow into an abuser. Speaking up could have had an influence in protecting them and scores of new victims from experiencing the same traumas, or God forbid, perpetuating those behaviors further still.

The tragic pattern reveals that celebrity status and the heat of a white-hot spotlight is exactly *why* these abuses and landmines are far less likely to be unearthed or reported. On the rare occasion someone is brave enough to do so, it's often shut down by a system of power and intimidation, or of sweeping things under the carpet to protect an image.

Sadly this is just as true in ministry as it is in the mainstream. A large number of stories go unspoken in church, simply because people are more afraid to talk about the taboo and compromise the whole house of cards, and these secrets end up causing way more destruction in the long run. That's the formula in every situation.

> *WE DON'T SPEAK UP BECAUSE WE THINK IT WILL BREAK SOMETHING—BUT NOT SPEAKING UP BREAKS EVERYTHING.*

We've seen this in many major ministries that occupy big platforms in the past few years. The only upside is that we're at a cultural crossroads, where we have an opportunity to continue the cycle or prayerfully scrutinize the very visible wreckage and learn how to catch it early or stop it altogether.

We do that in every other scenario. When there are fatalities associated with a particular car design, it's recalled, studied, rebuilt, and safety tested before it can be legally put back on the road. Companies even invest millions in researching ways to make cars safer for our pets.

We fail to do this same kind of important work where unspoken issues cause emotional and spiritual damage and injury. As Christians or leaders in the church, we're called to be hypervigilant in making sure eternal purpose is not quenched by eternity-stealing problems.

There was a documentary that came out in 2022 on the collapse of Hillsong Manhattan where author Elle Hardy[8] says of the tendency to stay silent in large ministries, "It is a culture of 'protect the brand at all costs' and whatever it takes to achieve that."[9] In reality (not to sound like a broken record, but I want to drive this point home), staying silent does the opposite. What could have been a lesson in authenticity, diligence, and purity—sending messages of redemption from the church and demonstrating how to put the Word into action—was silenced into irreparable damage. What someone could have exposed early on comes out later in a globally recognizable scandal that is derailing, disenchanting, and damaging to those who are watching and who are hit with the shrapnel. We're losing generations from what they see, hear, and experience of our failures.

## "US TOO"—WE'RE ALL IN THIS TOGETHER

As we dig deeper, you'll be surprised how consistent that "me too" response is. I've shared the story of sexual abuse with a babysitter and, as a result, repeating that behavior when I was not much older. At the age of ten, I didn't have the tools to process what had happened to me. Instead, I acted out what was done to me. We have to remember that children repeat behaviors they see; all abuse is learned. The statistics of

---

8. Elle Hardy, *Beyond Belief: How Pentecostal Christianity Is Taking Over the World* (London: Hurst, 2022).
9. *Hillsong: A Megachurch Exposed*. Breaklight Pictures. 2022.

how many have taken a deep, sharp inhale of surprise and recognition as they say, "The same happened to me—and I responded the same way too—and I've never said that out loud before," would surprise you. This confession is often met with an outpouring of tears—of relief, recognition, and rescue, evolving from and beyond the "Me Too movement," into an "us too" phenomenon. These heartbreaking yet healing discoveries have the ability to bring every human being behind them into the light and into next-level living.

Sometimes the secrets are ours. Sometimes they're secrets about others where we need to "see something, say something." Either way, we have a responsibility in most cases to break the bonds of going along to get along and name the issue. The Truth is the "in case of emergency" axe that can shatter the glass houses we're living in.

How do we handle this in our workspace, personal relationships, churches, homes, neighborhoods, schools, and communities at large? You'd think that's where it gets tricky, speaking up beyond ourselves, but it's really not. Speaking up is just unfamiliar and out of the ordinary in contemporary American culture. Once you learn the freedom of doing so, it's a game changer that finds its way into all our conversations and circles, from simple and superficial to complicated and consequential. It *changes everything*. Every issue needs voices to speak up about it in detail—people who aren't afraid to shape the health of these spaces for the sake of those who are in them.

The more I discovered these truths in the big places in my life, the more I realized how transformative they could be in the smaller spaces, and how easy. (Why do we make it so hard?!) On one of my son's teams there was a coach who had, let's say, an NFL vocabulary in a little league setting. There may be no crying in baseball, but there was plenty of sobbing here, and it was having an impact on some of the kids' self-image off the field.

Talk among the parents ranged from "He doesn't mean it; it's just how he talks" and "A little tough love won't hurt them" to "He needs to go." Implementing what I was learning ("field research" before I try it out on you), I simply…said something. A little Real Talk with the coach.

It turned out, he was incredibly appreciative. It actually was just the way he talked, which meant it wasn't an anger management issue or worldview that would take therapy to change. Awareness was the only tool he needed to be able to make an adjustment. It was all he knew.

> *WE ALL HAVE OUR EMOTIONAL, CULTURAL, OR HABITUAL "ACCENTS" THAT WE DON'T EVEN KNOW WE SPEAK WITH, AND WE JUST NEED A LITTLE "SPEECH THERAPY."*

That can happen when we have the heart to talk to one another.

That adjustment changed his relationships with parents and kids, as well as the development of the young athletes he was coaching. It might have changed his longevity in that position and even profession, and therefore his role and influence in the community. Once again, Real Talk changes everything.

Admittedly, that was an easy one compared to a lot of situations that are systemically broken, but if you want change in any setting, it starts with an individual. This applies to anyone, but it's "required living" for Christians. We're biblically called to speak up to one another.[10]

## REAL TALK CHANGES EVERYTHING

Imagine this illustration of a common concept in human behavior. There is no one on the dance floor. All it takes is one brave person,

---

10. Matthew 18:15 NLT: "If another believer sins against you, go privately and point out the offense. If the other person listens and confesses it, you have won that person back."

and they are soon joined by a group, and then it becomes a party. As a species, we follow what we see happening because it's safe and comfortable—we saw it worked for someone else and, therefore, we have *permission* to try it. That's the principle of how healing works through Real Talk.

The hashtag #Normalize (or #LetsNormalize) is capitalizing on this, paving the way for creating change in areas that we as a culture and society have come to accept or overlook. Pushing a disruptive conversation in a "speak up" direction normalizes what has previously landed anywhere from ignored to taboo. You can make yourself (your life, church, family) more bulletproof by normalizing tough conversations, changing the narrative, and bringing the contagiously negative out into the healing open.

I've been putting these principles to the test and into practice through Real Talk as an active leadership tool currently based in churches across the globe. Through the Real Talk process, we're test-driving the nuances of how to speak up better and get more people talking more easily. We're learning so much so fast that, frankly, it's why I started writing it down in this book.

We need a supersaturation of what people are learning *from each other* in Real Talk sessions in all of our societal environments, a new standard where we normalize the traditionally unspoken, buried, and avoided. We create space for the uncomfortable because that's where the enemy gets a foothold. I've watched C-level executives serving as Head of Culture create a bubble where employees can't talk about certain subjects seemingly out of "sensitivity to others" or leadership's directive to go the other way, but the results are a toxic work environment. That's the polar opposite of what is needed.

We also create spaces for silence in Real Talk. That may sound ironic, but it's the kind of crucial silence that allows for tears and provides the time and space for people to sit with their grief and to process their discovery that letting it out isn't breaking them—but it is breaking chains. We say, "Speak your secrets, name your chains, and watch them break in front of you." It's so important to honor this rare space and allow people to feel deeply and find their light, discovering their way along the path forward. This protects people from snapping back to their previous reality and reverting to the familiar habit of covering up. A quick recovery from a fresh vulnerability often leads to ignoring progress and pretending to be perfect again.

We don't have it all together. None of us do. No, not one. What we do have is the opportunity to be "silent no more." It's a tool God can use to work all things together for good,[11] allowing what was intended for evil to be used for good,[12] and for the truth to do what God's Word promises: set you free.[13]

## BRAVERY BEGETS BRAVERY

The most altruistic and impacting choice we can make is to throw open the doors and let light shine into every corner. Sharing the uncomfortable and even ugly parts of our stories is the most powerful gift we can offer one another.

That's one of the most beautiful things I've been able to witness firsthand with the work people are doing through Real Talk. It's the same work we're doing here in this book if you're ready to turn a page in your life: When you're brave enough to say it out loud, you give the next person permission and freedom to do the same. When one person says out loud what they think they can't, the next person learns they can. And then they do. And so on.

What did it take to open that dark room and begin to rebuild the brokenness? We just needed to talk about it. Say it out loud.

---

11. See Romans 8:28: "And we know that in all things God works for the good of those who love him, who have been called according to his purpose."
12. See Genesis 50:20: "You intended to harm me, but God intended it for good to accomplish what is now being done, the saving of many lives."
13. See John 8:32: "Then you will know the truth, and the truth will set you free."

## SPEAK THE UNSPEAKABLE.

What happens from there is moving, powerful, anonymous, and has endless potential to unlock doors, starting by unlocking the little rooms we've kept barred shut since the moment something happened to us. We breathe life into little broken pieces and grow them into new life. Instead of disease, we see them as seeds. We realize, in the right soil, we can be fully alive again.

Some are realizing for the first time how they have functioned as walking dead for most of their adult lives. A great phrase I heard from a father separated from his daughter that captures this feeling was, "I feel like I'm already dead and just haven't fallen over yet." Others have long dismissed these parts of themselves as okay to be dead.

It's not okay (we'll get into that more in chapter 3), which will be a recurring theme. I'll say this to you in every chapter, sometimes on every page, and we repeat it like a battle cry in every leader guide and video in the Real Talk sessions:

## IT'S NOT OKAY, AND YOU DON'T HAVE TO SETTLE FOR IT.

I'll say it until you say it. When you say it, someone else will be free to do the same, and so on, in an epidemic of freedom that *changes everything.*

This is why We Need to Talk.

So, let's talk...

# CHAPTER 2

# MADE FOR MORE, BUT WHO HAS TIME TO GET THERE?

The enemy wins in stealing our purpose before we even know
there is a battle.

Here's a question: If your children and grandkids got to live exactly the life you have lived from your own childhood until now, would you be willing to sign your name on that contract? The same communication skills, relationship types, self-image, sex life, secrets, ability to recognize abuse and speak up. Are your experiences what you would want for them? If you were paving the way for an identical life for them, would that give you hope or haunt you?

How you've felt internally your whole life. What you never spoke out loud. What you settled for, never solved, or took too long to address. What you did that no one else knew about, no one ever saw.

If they had the marriage you had, the love and communication with your spouse, the sex you have or don't have in your marriage or outside of marriage. Your level of transparency and comfort in your own skin.

The friendships in your life, past and present. The understanding and certainty of your purpose or your ability to chase it. Your integrity, how you do your job and how you deal with finances, both personally and in the workplace. Your faith and its development—how it started, how it's going, what you're able to do with your belief.

If everything in their life (or the rest of your life) was exactly as it has been so far, and that's all you desire for yourself or for them, then this probably isn't for you. But if there's something in you that knows you don't want your kids or grandkids to carry your same burdens—to walk with the same acceptable pattern of anger, bitterness, gossip, self-doubt, wounds, limitations—then we have work to do. The good news is, if you're willing, it's work that works, every time.

If not for your kids, then what about anyone in your sphere of influence—all of those God has put in your path and in your care? What are you passing on to the people who have passed through your life?

If not for others, then for you: Do you want the same road ahead for yourself that you've always walked? Is where you're standing where you want to stay? You might be longing for resounding change—even though you might be so beset with complacency that you think it doesn't matter, you'll just ride it out until you die. Just one more "what if" and we'll move from questions to the answers that are so within reach. *What if there was so much more?* What if you can't imagine what God has for you to be, or be free of, even if you only had a single day left to live?

## YOU'RE NOT JUST READING A BOOK

It doesn't matter where you are in life, how insurmountable the mountain in front of you, the setback or false starts, or the water under the bridge. Ask yourself if you want your next ten or twenty years to be the same as the last ten or twenty. Take the time here to pause and consider it seriously. Think about what you have in front of you and where you've been. This matters. You're not just reading a book for entertainment, you're making decisions. One way or the other, you're determining the path ahead of you—more of the same or making moves toward a way of living you've always wanted but didn't believe you could have. Whether small shifts or major redirections, this will change you.

Here's *why* this matters: It isn't just about being happy, feeling good, raising healthy generations. Those are valuable and desirable side effects, but the real power of the equation is bigger than any of this—bigger, probably, than you have any sense of. Beyond the scope of what you can see or guess, you were made for more, and you are more than able to get there.

If you're breathing, there's a reason. We are not accidental. We were knit together[14] with and for a purpose. It's one of the most recurring assurances in the Bible: that everyone, everywhere, has been created by God with a one-of-a-kind, eternal purpose. Why, then, are such a small percentage living in it (or living it out)?

You know the phenomenon when you repeat a word too many times and it loses its meaning? We're running that risk in this chapter (*purpose, calling, made for more*), but we're also running that risk in life. We repeat the idea on coffee cups and greeting cards: "You're special!" "No one else can do what you do!" until the words lose meaning. We're not taught enough that a divine intention for our life is a given, as nonnegotiable as our fingerprints and as timeless as the Creator who designed it and set it in motion. The Bible says God set the stars in their place[15]; how much more would He have placed you and established the light within you?

Get comfortable with the idea of divine intention and purpose, your reason for being. We're going to unpack it and position it, so you can pursue it. This is where you decide to move in a new direction and make a personal decision that you want more. There's always a cost. There

---

14. See Psalm 139:13: "For you created my inmost being; you knit me together in my mother's womb."
15. See Psalm 8:3: "When I consider your heavens, the work of your fingers, the moon and the stars, which you have set in place."

might be a sacrifice. There will most certainly be a change. Any time we learn something new, even for trivial interests or pastimes, we download a whole new set of tools and knowledge. We develop new habits, read different things, make peer connections with shared interests, and buy new "stuff" to use in pursuing our interest—biking, photography, golf, cooking. How much larger is the shift for something that could rewrite everything in your orbit? Remember, this work scales from the individual to the world stage.

Real Talk walks you through your personal, internal dialogue of the most intimate struggles.

Real Talk rewrites relationships and communication ability.

Real Talk is the shift in perspective we need in our institutions, especially how we function as the church.

When we say this changes everything, that means *everything*—nothing left unchanged—and if that's not worth the investment of your time and strength, what is? It's going to be the greatest and most important thing you've ever walked into, so it's going to require a little bit of work.

## YOU ARE HERE

I've spent years guiding groups, churches, individuals, and of course myself through this process. And let's be real—it has taken an army to guide me. I fully recognize that different people are coming into this conversation from different points of reference and readiness. Over the course of this chapter, we'll all pull together from our different points of view onto the same page, prepared for the work and positioned well within reach of results.

First, let's figure out where you're starting, so you have a better sense of where you need to go and how to get there:

Some are completely unfamiliar with the fact that if they're here, there's a reason, and that reason bears eternal weight: *"The idea of having personal purpose is entirely new to me."*

Some want purpose but are stuck on how to begin to identify much less pursue it: *"I've heard of it but don't know if I believe it—I've never felt I matter that much."*

Some know they have a purpose but feel they're coming up short in pursuit of it: *"I know I was meant for more, raised with a strong sense of worth and calling, but I don't know what mine is or how to get there, and even if I did, who has the time?"*

Some are thriving but wondering what's next: *"I feel I'm living my purpose, but is that it? Am I done, or is there more?"* Even at this very fulfilling phase, there's always more to find. If we're alive, at any age or stage, we can be sure God has more for us to do.

No matter which one you identify with most, the process for progress moves in the same direction and follows many of the same steps. It's a biblically based approach you can put into practice consistently throughout your spiritual development as you continue to level up and grow.

As we touched on briefly in the introduction to this book, this concept started in the small print on the back of business cards we created when I first started reaching out to women entrapped in the world of human trafficking. It grew from one of our first steps as a burgeoning organization searching for the most impacting way to make a meaningful connection and a memorable point. The message on one side read:

## *"EVER WONDER IF THERE IS MORE? ARE YOU READY?"*

At first, we assumed that part was stating the obvious, and the real work would come in providing these women tools to move into the "more" that God had for them. But we quickly discovered we had to step back to square one and introduce this concept as new information to most. Even for those who sensed that it was true, they had lost their sense of hope, the belief that more was within reach or that they deserved to fulfill a purpose—or to feel fulfilled.

I myself had carried that feeling around since birth—the absolute assurance that I was made for more. But even with that driving sense, I too was completely disconnected from how to get from point A to point "Be-loved." I was honestly too wounded from such a young age that I didn't know where to start or what to do, and even if I figured any of that out, I certainly didn't have time to do anything about it. I was too busy trying to stay alive and keep a flicker of hope. When I thought I was healed, I didn't know there was more; I was focused on other things.

My focus was how to make my life look perfect and camouflage the backpack of shame that was permanently fused to my shoulders. I knew God had invited me to take His yoke instead of mine and that His burden was light—but what does that even mean? And what good is that thought when I'm carrying some things that clearly are not "light"? How do you move from one place in life to another where that verse changes from inspirational cliché to the internally rewiring promise on which God intended for us to stand?

As I began to see the women's reactions to this invitation—from those who had never heard that hope before to those who had been trying to silence it in their heart for years—I realized two things, which put me on the path to ultimately creating the Real Talk program and writing this book:

This message was news to so many. We'd have to start at the foundation of this understanding.

This message isn't (shouldn't be) just for people in more obvious, trial-based lifestyles of tragedy and trauma (like the anti-human trafficking organization in which it began). It's for every single one of us.

Including myself. It was my own personal journey (from feeling to fulfilling; from fear to freedom; from pain to purpose) that built the tenets of Real Talk. Discovering my own freedom from speaking out, the wildfire effect of seeing others set free, and my own eternal purpose set me on the path of carrying this bullhorn to the nations. Only when I stepped out and began sharing the message did I learn it was the key to what's broken about our personal lives and faith as well as our communities and the worldwide church.

But we're getting ahead of ourselves. It's important to do this work in order, step by step, and not skip or rush any stage of development. Remember, you're not just reading a book; you're changing things.

## I HAVE A KEY FOR THAT

When I was a child, I already knew these doors were there to open. I was born with a sense that I was made for more, which made me feel like I was given an important cheat sheet. I couldn't sit still in my hunger to figure it out. Even as an adult, there was a fire burning under me—a sense that God wanted to leapfrog to another level of purpose that I hadn't yet found. I didn't want to follow my mother's path, or remain in the rut I was in.

When I came to each one of these doors, I felt blocked at first, but I also started hearing God say, "I have a key for that." For so long I didn't give Him full access to take me where He wanted to go because there were areas of my life I'd unknowingly hidden away and didn't want to, or couldn't, open to God. My history, my marriage, my shame. I wasn't ready. I was stuck.

There's a common illustration about how elephants in captivity are tied with a strong chain when they're young. They try and try to break free, but when they are unsuccessful, they quickly learn to think they aren't capable, until they no longer even try. That's why you can tie down even a full-grown elephant with a single, snappable rope. They have endless power and strength, but they let themselves be held in place by an insignificant prison. A lie that's no match for their true identity and ability, if only they knew the power they had within.

Sound familiar?

Realizing I was being held by these remnants of rope from throughout my past, the light started to come on that maybe I had the strength to get unstuck. Maybe I had the opportunity to move forward. Maybe I had the God-given ability to break free. Only God can make the impossible possible, but my hands were open, so I started to pull at the ropes and unravel the strings. That's when strongholds began to tear away like loose threads.

If someone is willing to say yes to just the very next step (whatever is next for you from where you stand), each step accomplishes exponentially more. Speaking the unspoken, doing the work to excavate, rewriting long-lived lies and trading them for light, laying down stepping-stones so others can follow in your footsteps—patterns begin to form that become easier to recognize and therefore easier to follow when you come to the next hill.

*YOU START TO TRADE:*
*WEIGHT FOR WORTH*
*ODDS FOR OPPORTUNITY*
*PROBLEMS FOR POWER*
*CONFLICT FOR CONFIDENCE*

Don't get me wrong—it's not always easy. With all this talk about "speaking up" being transformational, it can sometimes be brutal. It's worth the battle (I've never heard a single person say it wasn't worth it to take the hard steps), but here's the part you can especially take to the bank:

## STAYING IN THE PAST IS HARDER THAN GETTING PAST IT.

When you're dealing with secrets, you need to be prepared for the effect of the bold steps you're going to need to take. When I started with this message, some people hated me for it. They wanted the status quo—don't upset the apple cart, let sleeping dogs lie. Once you see the difference that happens when you move from the darkness of secrets and shame into the light of nothing to hide, you can't do it any other way. The cat doesn't go back in the bag.

You move from "Who has time for that?" "It's not the right time," "That would be too difficult, and I can't process that right now," to "There's no better time than now," "Time is of the essence," "It's crucial to do the right thing, right now, before one more day is lost running in the wrong direction." People might hate you for that too. These are hard first steps, and some are going to feel you're turning a mirror on their problems by changing yours. Stay the course. It's the only way we're going to get to the other side.

We'll talk more about *how* to stand strong in chapter 10, "No Going Back." One step at a time. For now, we have three important steps we're about to walk through together—and don't worry, we'll be filling a toolbox with exactly how to traverse this terrain. You're not alone; not only will I be with you every step of the way through this process, but so are the thousands of real people going through Real Talk as we lean on the wisdom, discoveries, and freedom they've already gained.

If you're working with a notebook, write these down as your *goals and benchmarks* and begin thinking through the unprocessed things from your past or present that come to mind when you read them, as well as what you want each of these milestones to bring as you move into your future:

Discovering your potential for *eternal* impact and the freedom of living in God's plan.

Excavating what might have stolen or blocked your calling.

Moving forward past bonds, boundaries, and battles to living abundantly blessed.

This is the point where you might be seeing some of your initial passion and motivation start to flicker as you start thinking less about reading and more about real life. But let me tell you, *if you're not letting someone speak truth to you, you're the scariest thing out there.* Living like that will keep you so far off the course of your purpose and calling it's literally dangerous.

There's a theory that if you ask at the end of any meeting, "Is there anything more?" the last 2 percent people have been holding on to is the main thing they came in with and, for whatever reason, left unsaid. Some of the reasons are strongly symbolic of why we do this in life (studying communication skills in a corporate setting as a microcosm of how we relate on a grander scale):

We're afraid of what others may think, say, or do in response.

We're afraid of looking stupid or being wrong.

We don't think what we have to say is important or is going to make a difference.

We just didn't take or make the time.

That 2 percent, though, might be the whole reason we're here.

This journey isn't a choice between status quo and bold goals. It's a journey between ultimate fulfillment versus falling utterly apart if you continue to leave these crucial spiritual foundations untended.

*IT'S TIME TO DECIDE:*
*ARE YOU GOING TO GO BACKWARD,*
*STAND STILL,*
*OR MOVE FORWARD?*

You know the phrase, "What have you got to lose?" If you think of what you can lose in terms of your fears, that might stop you here. But I dare you to flip that phrase around and think of it forward:

*WHAT HAS GOD GOT FOR YOU THAT YOU*
*STAND TO LOSE IF YOU STAY WHERE YOU ARE?*
*WHAT HAS HE PLANNED THAT YOU DON'T*
*WANT TO MISS OUT ON?*

Our unwillingness to clear out our spiritual attics and basements is a "no thank you" to God for the blessing and calling He's longing to realize in our lives. If you're okay with continuing to turn a blind eye to what you don't want to face (turning away from your purpose), you might as well stop reading and let this be your last chapter (pun intended). The door will seal itself shut in time.

If that's not okay—if you want more—then get ready, you're about to turn the corner.

> *"This third I will put into the fire; I will refine them like silver and test them like gold. They will call on my name and I will answer them; I will say, 'They are my people,' and they will say, 'The Lord is our God.'"* (Zechariah 13:9)

# CHAPTER 3

# EVERYTHING IS OFF

*This is the 911 call of the soul.*

I'm not okay. You're not okay. None of us are okay, and *that's not okay.*

The issue isn't just with us individually, and it's not just a personal problem involving our home or our families—it's affecting our world. It's systemic and at the heart of all our systems. Everything is off.

To understand this and begin to turn the battleship in an ocean of turmoil, we need to explore and embrace two revelations in one.

Calling brokenness what it is instead of hiding it and pretending everything's perfect

Accepting that this is not only normal (common, rampant), it's changeable, and urgent

Your response is what determines if things continue in the same, devastating direction or if you start to turn the wheel. Even one almost imperceptible inch in the direction of God's greater hope for you and for His church counts, because those turns have momentum and span huge distances over time. They're contagious and have the weight of the Word behind them. Can you feel the water shift beneath the ship even from the thought and hope that things could be different?

I'm going to keep reminding you that you're not just reading. If you take this walk in a Real Talk direction, you're changing the face of the future for yourself, your children, your family, your community. This work has the potential to change what's happening in our schools and in our local church. As we, together, *are* the church, that means we have our hand on the key that changes the church worldwide.

We spend our lives wearing a heavy cloak of reasons not to act—to stand still and do nothing, leave well enough alone, go along to get along. We function from a place of paralysis. Fears of reactions, loss, disruption, shame. It turns out, however, that we are experiencing a greater loss by standing still. Immobile and quiet. Incapacitated.

There's something hidden in the other side of that word—*incapacitated*—when we let God in and invite Him to turn it around: capacity. You have limitless capacity to change everything within your reach—and some things far beyond your reach or imagination.

To begin to make this turn, this change, we have to get honest about what we're facing and how much we're personally contributing to the problem.

Before we dive into a pivotal acceptance of a very big truth—a hard truth to some—let's check in with where we are in this journey:

We started out simply with the introduction of an idea that **we need to talk** and are welcome to—the gentle suggestion that you're not the only one, you're not alone, and if you're willing to step into the warm light of honesty and openness, you begin a move toward healing and purpose that sets you free and begins a domino effect. We took a tour through the overall idea of Real Talk and why it matters.

We unpacked that one of the core reasons it matters most is that you were **made for more**, and that the "more" in question isn't a small, finite, earthly idea, but tied to infinitely powerful reasons that you're here.

We'll take all of that further in chapter 9 when we're more equipped to peruse and pursue the fabric of your eternal purpose.

Now, we're rounding the bend on the "diagnosis" portion (Part One) in your Real Talk journey where we face the fact that *everything is off*. Admitting there is a problem, naming it, and by doing so, beginning to call it out into the light. We are not exposing ourselves to a spotlight of shame and embarrassment, but the exact opposite. We're pulling things out of the dark where the enemy wants them to fester and mold with the misinformation that you're not acceptable, that you're shameful, irredeemable. We're inviting one another to climb out from our cramped, trapped places where the "accuser of our brothers and sisters"[16] can keep us locked with his false description and verdict of our condition, separated from how God sees us and from what God can do through us in the bright light of day.

Remember those cards mentioned in the last chapter that we would hand out to sex trafficking victims, reminding them (or, in most cases, introducing them for the first time to the idea) that they were made for more? The front of the card asked a key question, one that's more weighted than many realize the first time they read it:

## "ARE YOU READY?"

Sometimes it would take two years to get a response, running after a girl who didn't believe she was made for more. Or others who believe there might be more but don't feel they will ever be able to access that opportunity, potential, or promise because of things that have happened in their lives. But land on that last word there—*promise*. There is a weaker definition where something "shows promise," which means

---

16. Revelation 12:10.

something or someone has "ground for expectation of success." But the primary definition of a promise, and the only definition of a biblical promise, is "a declaration that one will do or refrain from doing something specified," or a "declaration that gives the person to whom it is made a right to expect or to claim the performance or forbearance of a specified act."[17]

There is no "if" in that definition, but there are several absolutes—like a right to expect and claim the performance of a promise. Our response to God is part of the equation of actually living in His promises, but there is no question of whether or "if" He will fulfill what He promises. It is within reach to anyone—no matter what. Your circumstances only change your perspective; they cannot change your potential in a God-ordained purpose. Only God can open and close those doors. The question is whether you're willing to do the work it takes to walk through them—which can start with simply being able, willing, and free to talk through them.

## NOBODY'S TALKING ABOUT THIS

Here's where we're failing one another (and ourselves) as Christians and as the church. (I warned you that you were going to need to be "ready" for this part of the conversation. Time to gird up and move forward. He called us to feed His sheep, and the truth is, we've left each other in the dust.)

> *THE WAY WE TALK IN SOCIETY OR CHURCH DOESN'T ALLOW OR INVITE PEOPLE TO BRING THEIR HONEST NEED OR PROBLEM INTO THAT SOCIETY OR CHURCH.*

---

17. *Merriam Webster*, s.v. "promise," https://www.merriam-webster.com/dictionary/promise.

In our homes, jobs, small groups, cathedrals, Facebook comments, and friendships, we're telling people the opposite of the truth of the gospel, before they even think of coming to us, or to church, or to the heart of Jesus.

We talk a lot about spiritual growth, but we're not being honest about how to get there.

## WE DON'T TALK ABOUT PURGING THE HIDDEN, RAW BROKENNESS THAT KEEPS US FROM MOVING FORWARD.

We are not providing the next steps to inner healing that will help every person reach their purpose and help future generations do the same by giving them examples of success and permission (instead of prohibition) of what needs to be done—taboo steps of blunt honesty and transparency—to become whole.

The work of Real Talk and the work you're doing right now in reading this is part of a scriptural, biblical process of spiritual healing that has fallen entirely out of the discipleship process and adult education curriculum in Christian teaching materials. Nobody's selling the whole package; it's nonexistent.

We're not only *not* talking about it; we're silencing those who try. Why? It will upset others. It will embarrass the family. Damage the brand. Hurt someone's feelings.

Here's the truth: Others are already upset. Our families are already embarrassed and will be more so when they fall apart. We live as the broken shells we've become because hurt people hurt people. The "brand" of the banners of our churches is demolished when "another pastor" is exposed for whatever failing—sexual misconduct, misuse of funds, drugs, alcohol, perpetuating abuses in the church by staying quiet about it, or burying the truth.

We "hush" our problems within the church—don't talk about it, don't report it, don't address struggles honestly *especially* in leadership, for fear of retribution and ending our ministry—but then it always comes to light, and the world is waiting to say, "See? That's Christians for you. That's why I don't go to church. That's why I don't believe in God." Then we fail publicly, epically, and we fuel their "that's why" with diesel.

That's why. We're why. How we're living. How we're responding. How we're hiding what God wants us to bring into the light and exactly what God wants us to bring *to* church. That's the one part we leave home, because we're being *told* to.

We don't know and aren't teaching the hard and helpful steps to inner healing, specifically for things we're afraid to bring up and out. We have forgotten (or abolished) the simplicity of the keys to spiritual growth that will help people reach their purpose, become who they were created to be—beloved, intentional, known, called, destined, loved— and get future generations to do the same.

A right faith is being undone today by the idea of "faith" that's being put forward in the identity of contemporary faith or westernized Christian culture.

We want an altar-call experience, but we don't want to admit what we need to admit, at that altar, for emotional, mental, spiritual cleansing. In some cases, we're embarrassed or ashamed. But here's an even bigger, systemic problem that will require us to challenge church culture: We're not being honest enough about what sin is. We've begun to teach our kids, and to believe ourselves, that the broken parts of us are just the new normal. We're not admitting that everything is off.

On the contrary, we're saying, "Nothing's wrong," but we're not very convincing. You can see in the twitch of the eye and the pain in the smile that we don't believe that lie ourselves. But we're doing very little to change it. We're doing almost nothing at all. Worse than nothing—we're shoveling more dirt on top of the grave where we've buried the truth that was meant to set us free.

## DYING OFF THE VINE

We've normalized the work of the enemy and accepted this as a way of the world. We're out of alignment with the fruits of the spirit and have traded them for what turns out to be fruits of the enemy, once you take off the shiny packaging of, "It's just a joke," "It's just a TV show," "I don't have to go to church to be a Christian," "If it makes you happy, do it."

We've lost our connection to God's power when we live like this or build our churches on this sandy ground.[18] We're fruit off the vine. Picture that. We may look normal when we first fall away, but it's short-lived and far from the thriving for which we were born. We're not reaching for that hope, and worse, we're teaching others not to either. Together, we're dying off the vine.

We're busy yelling "stop abortion" while people are so wounded that they're not anywhere near being able to see the brokenness of abortion. We're not having the right conversation—or maybe we're having conversations out of order. Jesus began with relationship. He began with breaking bread, spending time, inviting in, or running to, all while living in and sharing Truth, by being Truth Himself.

He did this by showing up where people were—not just geographically, but emotionally, mentally, and spiritually. He loved others in moments of violent anger, betrayal, denial, doubt, arrogance, immoral relationships, adultery, prostitution. God healed sins before bodies. He

---

18. See Matthew 7:24–27.

healed hearts before providing for earthly needs.[19] He sat at the table again and again and loved the people at it, even the ones who would betray Him with a kiss.[20] Only in that relationship was He able to be the Word and build the foundation of the church on earth.

The church has been so focused on spreading what we see as the finite message of the gospel, attempting to meet more understandable needs like feeding the hungry, that we have not paid attention to the broken among us. People come to us for help and healing, and we hand them a Bible and tell them to go find someone to serve. We quickly shift them to being externally focused when they still have so much brokenness inside.

On the rare occasions someone tries to be open about the sin they battle, we shut it down saying it's "not Christian" or they need to "step out of ministry," which is usually code for "leave the church." It's true that the Bible says those who preach and teach are called to a higher standard,[21] but how do we maintain that standard if we aren't allowed access to confession and healing for the darkest parts of our struggle? When this is what we find in the church or from one another as Christians, it's no wonder people stop coming to a Christian space with their sin. If they don't come to us and to God, where is there left to turn?

The world welcomes them with open arms. No wonder they choose the world. We even expel well-established Christians within the church for their sin instead of working *through* their sin to help them excel in Christ.

## JUDGMENT VERSUS EXPOSURE

When I was in leadership in the church, I was aware of other leaders struggling with porn, justifying buying sex, and having affairs or being

19. See, for example, Matthew 9:1–8.
20. See Luke 22:48: "But Jesus asked him, 'Judas, are you betraying the Son of Man with a kiss?'"
21. See James 3:1: "Not many of you should become teachers, my fellow believers, because you know that we who teach will be judged more strictly."

emotionally involved with each other. The façade of marriage in the church is just as rampant as it is in the world.

Christians are turning to pharmaceuticals more than faith (acknowledging the legitimacy in some cases, but there are many cases of chemical escape more than medical need). Seventy percent of the people I have encountered and worked with in the church are involved with some level of abject sin.

Even seemingly simpler crutches like how much time is spent on social media platforms, distractive placebos for what we were hardwired to long for, are ways we fall short of God's plan for our lives. We reach for our smart phones an average of 2,600 times a day longing for—something.[22] But we're unable to translate that longing back to our Creator who's longing for us. We're losing our spiritual instinct, especially among younger generations. If we're so prevailed upon by alternate voices, how are we ever going to hear His voice break through?

While you're reading this, my guess is you're having one of two first-impression reactions:

## YOU'RE EITHER JUDGING OR EXPOSED.

If you can't understand what some struggle with and how it's possible to fall into certain sin, you've likely already passed judgment. You're appalled, disheartened, feeling hopeless about the state of the church. "That's why I don't go anymore." "Typical."

If you're relating, because you've been battling a story of your own that you feel you could never be transparent about, here's a quick

22. Julia Naftulin, "Here's how many times we touch our phones every day," Insider, July 13, 2016, https://www.businessinsider.com/dscout-research-people-touch-cell-phones-2617-times-a-day-2016-7.

question: Do you feel scared and called-to-the-carpet, or do you feel relieved that you could be understood and loved? Do you recoil at the thought of rejection, or is there a little lift at the idea that you're not the exception, you're not a monster, and that there actually is a clear path to becoming whole?

"Everybody's doing it" is not an excuse, but realizing that "everybody is doing it" means (read this slowly and let it sink way, way in): You. Are. Not. Alone. That's not a platitude, bumper sticker, or catchphrase you'll hear ad nauseum as we continue (though it's also all three). It's a hand of rescue and recognition. The thing you think can or will take you down also belongs to your co-laborer.[23] You may be hiding from shame, self-harming physically or emotionally, while, ironically, you're sitting next to others involved with the same struggles or worse. Your vocality could change everything in your own story—and theirs.

It doesn't matter what we're using to numb, it's all equal at the foot of the cross. Whether we're trying to avoid porn, alcohol, disordered eating, a shopping addiction, or sex outside of marriage, we all fall short, and God's Word says, "For whoever keeps the whole law but fails in one point has become guilty of all of it."[24] We're all completely guilty if we're not completely perfect, and there's only One who is.

First John 1:8–10 KJV puts it in plain English (or Greek): "If we say that we have no sin, we deceive ourselves, and the truth is not in us. If we confess our sins," which we'll get to in a couple chapters, "he is faithful and just to forgive us our sins, and to cleanse us from all unrighteousness. If we say that we have not sinned, we make him a liar, and his word is not in us."

If we say we have not sinned, we make the "author and perfector of faith"[25] a liar, and we say it every day through what we don't say. We send the message that everyone else is broken, but we have it all together.

---

23. See 1 Corinthians 3:9: "For we are co-workers in God's service; you are God's field, God's building."
24. James 2:10 ESV.
25. Hebrews 12:2.

We act like broken lives have no place in the church and only seemingly on-target Christians belong. We lead like we can do no wrong and teach others to shoot for the goal of our often weak façade.

## SHAMEFULLY SILENT

I saw it the most when I was in ministry, but I still see it today through Real Talk from all sides of the church aisle or platform: people who have been hurt by their experiences in church as congregations or staff; people in leadership who aren't being transparent about struggles or sin and believe they can't be, because of the reaction or perceived damage.

The truth is, greater damage is done in silence. Silence does greater damage to the individual who has no recourse or path within the ministry to get right with God, to the leader who is spiritually more accountable according to the Word, most often adding to their sense of guilt and shame, and to those outside the church who are watching us as our testimony as the church and body of Christ falls apart. This has always been the case, and we've done nothing to fix it in the contemporary church. But it's getting worse. If we don't build off-ramps where sin can be dealt with openly, relentlessly, and hopefully in today's Christian church, where will we go from here? Where is left for people to turn? The World is the only answer available currently—and the World is not a good answer.

We're not functioning from a place of compassion for a world that's not going to respond to judgment and is crying out to be loved. Jesus was unapologetic about the truth and unwavering—but only after He first met sinners where we were. He called for rocks to be laid to rest and said, "Neither do I condemn," before He said, "Go, and…sin no more."[26] He said, "Father, forgive them"[27] while they spat on Him as He carried the cross for our sake. He loved first. He led with the cross.

---

26. John 8:11 ESV: "She said, 'No one, Lord.' And Jesus said, 'Neither do I condemn you; go, and from now on sin no more.'"
27. Luke 23:34: "Jesus said, 'Father, forgive them; for they do not know what they are doing.' And they divided up his clothes by casting lots."

He chose each disciple, knowing He'd be denied, doubted, disappointed, betrayed. He calls us, then names us friend, brother, beloved, even knowing everything we've done, things we've never admitted or haven't yet given up. Things we're doing now and those we've yet to do. If we treated one another with this invitation of possibility, how different would our church function? How healthy would our families be? How hopeful would our world be?

## GREEN-LIGHTING SATAN

**Normalized:** We've normalized the work of the enemy, and the church has accepted it as "the way of the world." It is exactly that, but it's far from harmless, as we'd like to fool ourselves into believing. Satan, according to God Himself, is walking in the world with all his power and drawing prime attention, while our Father is from another kingdom and calling us into that security and perfection. If there is not horrendous grief for this danger and loss, a sounding of alarm for this tragedy, then we've declined the most beautiful and hard-won gift and abandoned the neighbor we were called to love as ourselves. This is the 911-call of the soul.

**Mainstream:** Satan has taken over as mainstream. His ways are more acceptable even among Christians than what God calls us to. Prayer is out of schools entirely. Satanic clubs are greenlit, yet if you want a Christian club, there are cases where they're required to have a non-Christian group leader for diversity. The devil is publicly popular while the church is moving underground.

**Thriving:** Did you know the Satanic Temple is thriving in America? Anything resembling satanism used to be an underground movement, clandestine and hidden. Now it's a denomination, and it's incorporating. In 2023, the Satanic Temple launched a "telehealth abortion clinic" in Albuquerque, New Mexico, that they are hailing as "the world's first-ever religious abortion clinic." This is not fake news.

**Pervasive:** Demonic activity is pervasive, but we no longer call it demonic activity—we call it our right. We've come—many of us unwittingly—into agreement with things that are not of God. I say this gently but urgently: If they're not of God then, by definition, they're of the enemy. Which means we are standing in agreement with Satan's desires. Basic transitive law—if A equals B, and B equals C, then A equals C. If Satan is against God, and we make a choice that's against God, then our choice, our will, is equal to the enemy's will. That's pretty hard-hitting, but it needs to be said in a world where we're growing so soft. We're caught between two extremes.

We're not hard-hitting enough, safe in our watered-down bubbles.

And we're too hard-hitting, not showing up for some who need a touch of God's authentic presence in their lives.

We're in the middle—a very lukewarm center where no part of this equation is working. Good for nothing. The opposite of aligned with His will—spewed out.[28]

When we're standing in this place and serving the world from it, what are we serving? We're trading the fruits of the spirit for the rotting fruits of the enemy. We trade the potential for lives filled with love, joy, peace, kindness, faithfulness, and the like for results like fear, anger, bitterness, resentfulness, and insecurity. We allow ourselves to be pulled on daily by the forces of anything that goes against self-control, controlled instead by urges of lust, greed, infidelity, and insecurity. Out of control. We think we're the faithful, but we're having bad-apple effects.

Normalized, thriving, pervasive, mainstream—things we cannot say about the church on earth today. We've grown quiet, but Satan has grown loud. He is present and active in lives and in our culture and community, while the church is going into hiding or changing clothes to suit the mood. We don't want to offend. We started trying to be P.C., which led to us becoming M.I.A.

---

28. See Revelation 12:15.

## THE CHURCH NEEDS A NEW MARKETING TEAM. OUR BRANDING AND MESSAGING IS DATED.

Satan is dominating market shares.

Because of this, the world is longing for acts of power. No one is seeing genuine, strong acts of the Holy Spirit. So they're filling the void with power wherever power offers a forgery—fake forms. People are flocking to psychic coaches, starved for someone who can tell them "in the spirit" (in *a* spirit) who they are and why they're here. The problem is, they're finding revelation and divination that are not of God, the true Holy Spirit. There's a whole spiritual realm—a world of spirits—and God spent time in His Word warning us that the prince of darkness has spirits everywhere, roaming back and forth "looking for someone to devour."[29]

## SPIRITUAL COUNTERFEITS

Spiritual presence is there to be found—depending on where you're looking. You can call on "the spirits" and get an answer or hear something from the spiritual realm. It might even be close to true because it's trying to look as believable and desirable as possible. Remember, the enemy believes in God and knows how to quote Scripture, and he's going to present a beautifully packaged fabrication.

It's so hard to detect because of one of the most heartbreaking, simple reasons:

---

29. 1 Peter 5:8: "Be alert and of sober mind. Your enemy the devil prowls around like a roaring lion looking for someone to devour."

*SO FEW OF US KNOW WHAT AN IMITATION LOOKS LIKE BECAUSE WE KNOW SO LITTLE ABOUT WHAT GOD'S TRUE POWER LOOKS LIKE.*

We quickly accept the counterfeit.

But Satan knows. He knows what God's power is, and that we're so far from recognizing it in its fullness. He takes advantage of that with a full awareness that we're sheep who have wandered onto the rocks far from any memory or understanding of a flock. He works to get us to flock to him, and we do. We want to belong, and he's turned this into a gang war.

The enemy was a fallen angel who was the highest of the high—alluring, beautiful, envious. He wanted to be God, and he still does. He wanted everyone to follow him, and he still does. That's what he's working on every day: getting people to follow him and to want to go his way. Stealing worship with his spiritual counterfeit.

By definition, the word *counterfeit* means there *is* a real thing he's trying to emulate and ultimately match. That real thing is the answer that we center on in Real Talk. The power and person of Christ and His grace-filled presence and perfection are the only way we're going to get free of the things that hold us back and threaten to tear us apart.

It took time for our way of life to get this broken, but the good news is, though the systemic issues will take time to fix, the Holy Spirit can start the work of reconnection instantly and make His power available immediately to those who wish to confess and be healed.[30]

People are begging for an answer in their quest for self-understanding, asking the world, "Who do you see or say that I am?" We ask the

30, See James 5:16.

world for validation without understanding that our sense of being and belonging rests not in their answer to us, but in *our* answer to the same question Christ asks of us in Matthew 16:15: "Who do you say I am?"

Everything is off. It's true. But if our answer to that question is like Peter's in the Bible ("Simon Peter answered, 'You are the Messiah, the Son of the living God'"[31]), that should mean we believe in the promises tied to that confession. That faith walk works in both directions—promises that bring us into healing, and calling where we're *expected* to love our neighbor, which often looks different than we imagined. It's hard work. Author Bob Goff often covers this paradox in his books. In *Love Does*, he explains that loving your neighbor requires "sacrifice and commitment,"[32] and in *Everybody, Always*, he backs up this point by writing, "Sadly, whenever I make my opinions more important than the difficult people God made, I turn the wine back into water."[33]

Don't reverse the miracle—be the miracle; be the one who notices that everything's off and begins to work at turning just one thing on again. If we charge into Real Talk with each other, if we're willing to do the work, to let Him work through us, that's the key that changes everything. I've seen it with my own eyes. I've lived it. I can't be quiet about inviting you to live it too.

---

31. Matthew 16:16.
32. Bob Goff, *Love Does: Discover a Secretly Incredible Life in an Ordinary World* (Nashville: Thomas Nelson, 2012).
33. Bob Goff, *Everybody, Always: Becoming Love in a World Full of Setbacks and Difficult People* (Nashville: Thomas Nelson, 2018).

# PART 2:

# REVEAL

# CHAPTER 4

# EVERYONE HAS SECRETS

The average person keeps approximately thirteen secrets at a time, five of which they have never told another soul. The most common secrets include sexual behaviors and lies.[34]

O*ne in three women reports being sexually abused as a child. Of that group, over 90 percent knew their abuser well. Think of that.* Less than 10 percent of sexually abused children are abused by a stranger.[35] For everyone else, they were in a safe place, with a trusted companion, and had no clue that everything they thought about life, themselves, and the world was about to change.

Escalating this tragedy further, these numbers are just one round of the cycle of abuse. They don't account for what happens next. The experience of being sexually abused changes a child's worldview, self-image, and interaction with others, putting them astronomically more at

---

34. In a study by Columbia University reported in Michael Slepian et al. The experience of secrecy. *J Pers Soc Psychol.*, 2017 Jul;113(1):1-33. doi: 10.1037/pspa0000085. Epub 2017 May 8.
35. YWCA, "Child Sexual Abuse Facts," YWCA.org, September, 2017, *https://www.ywca. org/wp-content/uploads/WWV-CSA-Fact-Sheet-Final.pdf.*

risk to repeat the behavior and either be victimized again, or victimize another as a learned behavior.

Beyond exclusively sexual abuse, the percentage increases by the tens, with 60 percent of adults reporting abuse or other traumatic family circumstances during childhood. These scars carry into adulthood largely unaddressed. Of the few working through their issues, even fewer are taking that work or truth into the church. We're not showing up as the family God calls us to be to one another. Instead, we send a strong message that others would be chastised or shut down if they came to us or to the church, creating a culture of silence and perpetual brokenness. If an abused person is more likely to enter an abusive relationship, then they also pass that tendency on to their children, who will probably repeat the cycle again if not escalate it.[36]

You can do the math. The numbers make it clear how this influences the state of the world and of the church. The stats are staggering. That's part of the "white-hot why" behind Real Talk and why this work is so essential: Abuse breeds from one person's crisis to a global pandemic of emotional and spiritual disease and destruction. It's a wildfire, and wildfires can turn fast, always with total devastation in their path.

The other side of that "why" was my front-row seat, as I witnessed the light of hope come on in others' long-dark hearts when, as we touched on earlier, they first realize they're not the only one and they're not broken beyond repair.

## THERE'S A KEY

I spent so many years carrying around my backpack of shame and working overtime to live a perfect-looking life. And I was nailing it, let me tell you. I was willing to keep every part of my heart heavy and

---

36. According to a report by the Centers for Disease Control and Prevention, "Females exposed to child sexual abuse are at 2–13 times increased risk of sexual violence victimization in adulthood. People who experienced child sexual abuse are at twice the risk for non-sexual intimate partner violence." See "Child Sexual Abuse," CDC, updated April 6, 2022, https://www.cdc.gov/violenceprevention/childsexualabuse/fastfact.html.

broken, as long as it stayed hidden as well. I had no reason to believe there was any other way. I quite honestly had grown so used to it that I truly didn't believe I had anything wrong. All my issues had become normalized. No one told me—no one unearthed the unspoken things happening. Recovering from that vacuum of need, I now live every day making sure I've told someone—a single stranger or an entire nation—that *there's a key.*

## A KEY THAT OPENS DOORS YOU THOUGHT YOU COULDN'T BUDGE.

A key that locks doors behind you, cutting off demons that need never have access to you again.

We've explained this before, and I'll say it again, because this is the frame that became Real Talk realizations. Three contrasting cultures I moved through in the three major phases of my career showed me the effects of three different approaches to openness and authenticity:

The secular marketplace in metropolitan Chicago had no secrets and no shame. Nothing was hidden—but only because darkness was embraced and celebrated.

In a major ministry with a national spotlight, suddenly everything was hidden. How can you be transparent that you're struggling with your marriage while leading others in theirs, much less confess deeper sins and issues?

Serving in the world of sex trafficking with both the buyer and the victim—nothing was hidden again, by definition, but this time it was a world that ran on a currency of shame on both sides, and without the economy of hope.

## THE SAME KEY WORKS IN ALL THOSE DOORS—BUT NO ONE HAD IT IN HAND.

The beginning of my understanding of this—what was missing and what was needed—was me asking the questions at each turn: Why were things the way they were, and why wasn't anyone doing anything?

Back in the early days working in television and radio, I would ask myself, "How can all of this be going on and no one seems to care?" When I moved into ministry, the question was one I asked myself: "How long can I hold it together in a culture of silence; how can I keep up the façade? Why won't anyone escalate what is happening?" The fact was, I couldn't; they couldn't. Here I was, though, walking people through problems I hadn't yet begun to face myself.

I got my master's in clinical psychology and was working with a wide variety of individuals. Every patient presents differently, so we were trained to look at things as symptoms of a core issue that needs to be determined:

- A beautiful housewife from the North Shore who can't stop shopping
- A schizophrenic young man being released from prison on the west side of Chicago
- A young girl from downtown with an eating disorder
- A man who hates how addicted he is to porn

The common thread in every case was abuse—verbal, sexual, physical, alcoholism in the home, things that we're made to normalize as children. We watched these ways of living that we grew up thinking were normal—speaking a certain way, navigating beatings, showing love, managing discipline.

If someone says they have an issue with rage, we often discover that they were beaten as a kid as "discipline." Rage was normalized as an acceptable response. But we know instinctively as humans that it's *not* healthy. We know when something's not right. We don't often pay attention to *why* it is the way it is, why we are the way we are, and that there are things we can do to rewrite the script. Announcement: Our brokenness, our issues, our "ways," are not a given. They're surprisingly redeemable.

In my ministry life, I felt I had to present a perfect picture from the platform. (Think of how many feel like that in ministry or in the public eye and how that affects their leadership.) I really convinced myself I didn't have secrets. I was speaking, teaching, and leading small groups with intimacy as the Director of Training and Equipping. I was leading others to lead others. I displayed perfect on perfect on perfect. Broken begetting broken.

Deep down, maybe I knew I was hiding, pretending perfection, while I was encouraging everyone else to come out of hiding. I was holding on to shame—both from the past and from how I was living at that time, but it was deeply buried—while teaching others to step out of theirs and live free. I hadn't even discovered yet what free really was.

I believed I was helping, and hopefully I was, in part, but I also knew without a shadow of a doubt that I was not being fully authentic. There was a level of discontent. I was clearly made for more. There was a purpose far beyond anything I was doing, had done, or could do in my limited frame. I was unsettled because I could feel what was missing. I could feel the potential. But I had no idea where to begin.

## THE ROAD TO REAL TALK

Then I ended up in a confession session with a Catholic priest in a highly visible setting among perfectly polished friends, in front of whom I did not want to appear imperfect in any way.

*IT WAS AN UNLIKELY SCENARIO, AND ONE THAT UTTERLY TRANSFORMED MY LIFE WHEN I WAS INVITED TO SPEAK THE UNSPEAKABLE—A PIVOTAL ENCOUNTER THAT SET ME ON A JOURNEY TO DISCOVERING MY PURPOSE, MY LIFE'S WORK, AND WHAT YOU'RE READING HERE.*

We'll get to the specifics of that story in a bit, but what it did was bring all of my secrets to the surface where I had to face them, where I couldn't avoid them. I uncovered burdens I'd buried and forgotten and realized the eternal potential of breaking free of them. It was the key to the pattern of the spiritual freedom we're missing as individuals and in today's global church. It was the beginning of the road that became Real Talk.

But one thing at a time. So far, we've established that everyone has secrets and that speaking openly about them both disarms them and delivers you from their grasp. But I haven't told you mine yet, and *my secrets are why I know all of this, and why I want to speak the unspeakable for the sake of others.*

Remember, as you read my confession, that this was me who:

Didn't even fully realize I wasn't being authentic. My life struggles had become so normalized in my marriage and self-image that I didn't even realize how unreconciled I was or how far short I fell of the image I presented publicly.

Knew I had some buried failures and pains—things I didn't want to bring up or make known—but didn't think of them consciously as secrets like other people had.

Didn't think I had "real" secrets. After all, I was successful, married, a mom, a leader, financially comfortable, and threw the best children's birthday parties (my dad used to say every time he came to our house for an event it looked like he had stepped into a true circus. We even hosted annual luaus complete with hula dancers and flame throwers). Surely living a life of secrets doesn't look like that, right? Secrets are darker histories that create visibly broken lives, are they not?

They are not.

## MY SECRETS WERE LEGION

When I was young, my sister was killed. You hear of horrible accidents in families and the impact of those accidents in small communities like ours where everyone knows each other. But I lived it. It was not only the loss of someone I needed but the impact of growing up in the resulting environment, the dysfunction it left behind, and what I became in that space.

I was the youngest, so I took it all in and held it, observed without being supported. It led to me feeling invisible. It's no wonder I became the therapist, always available to hear what's going on and provide support to others unidirectionally. But I wasn't equipped to do that as a kid without it stripping things away from my development and functionality.

A few years later, I was molested on the way to church in what used to be a safe and trusted relationship. It happened with a family friend, but that's not even the worst of it. It happened in his truck, and when it was over, without saying a word, he grabbed his guitar, walked into the church, and led worship. I was a child in shock, and I cried in the bathroom, alone and changed at the hands of the person behind the music I could hear through the walls—the music that used to be my great joy. In tears and utter invisibility. No one knew. Secrets took root. I never went back to that church, and pay attention to this: No one ever asked why.

Silence made secrets take root, choking off a part of my spirit and my potential, were it not for the redeeming work God would later do. By the grace of God, it did not permanently steal my purpose. The Holy Spirit's promise to work all things together for good[37]—even what the enemy intended for evil[38]—would ultimately fuel my purpose. But I lived under decades of spiraling destruction before that wound would be turned toward the light.

It wasn't the only time I was molested. It happened prior to that with a close female, which created even more confusion and self-blame or self-judgment, especially for a young person who has no one to talk to. Identity comes into play early. When I later enacted this same behavior because it's what I knew, I was unknowingly perpetuating a very common cycle of children who are abused acting out in the way they're abused.

The cycle not only goes forward, it goes backward as well, which I wouldn't learn until my mother was in her eighties when she opened up her own cache of secrets and let me know it was her pain too. She was abused and didn't know how to talk about it or how to ask if something had happened to me. She didn't know how to find her own freedom or protect us from the same fate. She didn't have the tools for escape, protection, or change. She didn't know the way.

This is why we're here. To make a way. For you, the generations who brought you here, and the generations you can influence and lead in a more perfect Way.

We're not even out of my childhood yet. When I tell you I had secrets, they were legion. Experience tells me that, as I'm telling you what they are, several of you are reading this feeling the relief of relatability. Like so many have said—like we've said earlier in these pages—"I thought I was the only one." No matter your story, you're never going to be the only one.

---

37. See Romans 8:28.
38. See Genesis 50:20.

What happened in my younger years, combined with the cultural nature of my family, where women were meant to be seen as sexually appealing even at a young age, led to teenage years that were not only promiscuous, but that promiscuity put me at great risk that led to repeated sexual assault and later to an abortion I wouldn't share for years.

When I met and married my first husband, it's understandable that I accepted behavior in the relationship that was unhealthy and out of the ordinary. I was settling for what I had normalized since youth. I didn't believe anything better really existed; this was the only world I had known.

All of this and more came pouring out in a single night of prayer, confession, and healing that we'll really unpack in chapter 5, "The Lost Art of Confession." But it wasn't just about that one moment, it was about the years that followed and the ability to do the work that was needed. We'll cover the whole process—confession, healing, walking out your encounter, unleashing your purpose.

The step we're on is simply exploring and accepting the fact that there *are* secrets that we have to be willing to bring into the light. Being open to facing yours is where everything begins—being encouraged that you can survive and handle them with God's strength and, in doing so, you can find release and the most fulfilling purpose.

Right now, you and I are at the beginning of that road.

We've spent some time *"receiving"* (Part One) the basic information on what Real Talk is and why it matters, that you matter and are made for more, and that the way we're living now is not okay. Even for that very small percentage of readers who feel their life is pretty tacked down, we likely can all agree that the church is primarily in crisis, so even if the only reason you're chasing healing is for others' sake, it's still worth every one of us chasing it.

Now we're half-way through the process of *"revealing"* (Part Two), being true to facing our own secrets and the importance of bringing them to light and speaking the unspeakable.

Where we'll go from there will require the ability to walk out some difficult but powerful steps and to keep walking it out without turning back.

Whatever your secrets, they're the pressure point that's forming your diamond characteristics. That's what we have going on with people who are going through the Real Talk pathways. We see it every day. Having an encounter and processing this path with one person helps shine one facet of the jewel of who you are—and then you pivot and have a new session where you work with another person, who likely shares some commonality with your story. That person completes the cycle of purpose by proving to you that you're not the only one and you're strong enough to help others by your example of strength, honesty, and not being afraid of your secrets any longer.

It's a revealing process, and as you go forward, you're able to see clearly all the cuts that make you this reflective gem, unique and perfected. Each time this happens, it adds more dimension, light, depth, and beauty—that's how we're supposed to walk this out.

When you share the things you survived, rather than avoiding or hiding, you create offramps through speaking the unspeakable that reveal and reflect the perfection we were meant to become *in* Christ and *to* and *for* one another—people created by God who are living, breathing, amazing creatures with so many dimensions to us. When you begin to say what you haven't said before, truth begets truth, and good begets good.

Everyone has secrets. Will yours be the straitjacket that holds you back from the reach you were born to have—or will they be a tool that unearths a bed of spiritual diamonds? It depends on what you do with them. Will you let them fester? Or will you speak them into a most useful, powerful, purposeful existence?

# CHAPTER 5

# THE LOST ART OF CONFESSION

The risk is worth the reward. Do it scared.

The value of a biblical truth through the power of confession has all but lost its place in our society, the Church (capital C), and our individual faith. The word itself makes most cringe with anxiety, outside of confidential confessional settings like the Catholic Church, counseling, or conversations with your lawyer. Normalizing these unspoken conversations can disarm the often-false fear of "what would happen if people found out" and put us in contact with all God intended when He called us to repentant prayer, confessing your sins to one another.[39]

Confession is scary word. But it's just sharing your story. It can be that simple. Depending on how serious your story is, however, simple can still be scary, so we avoid it for a variety of reasons—not the least of which is the imaginary blowback of what we think would happen "if people only knew." If we don't think it's important or useful, and we

---

39. James 5:16: "Therefore confess your sins to each other and pray for each other so that you may be healed. The prayer of a righteous person is powerful and effective."

think it's a scary step, why would any of us pursue it? Just like that, it all but disappears from the culture of the Christian faith.

*Confession* is a foreign word. Many contemporary Protestant Christians see it as an element exclusive to the Catholic faith. The Code of Canon Law for the Catholic Church describes the practice officially, saying, "A member of the Christian faithful is obliged to confess in kind and number all grave sins committed after baptism and not yet remitted directly through the keys of the church nor acknowledged in individual confession, of which the person has knowledge after diligent examination of conscience."[40]

With the theological differences between the Protestant and Catholic faiths surrounding the organized practice of shared confession, it has slipped into the identity of something that either doesn't exist for non-Catholics, or is exchanged for private, personal confession between the individual and Christ. But confessing our sins "one to another"[41] is in the Bible, and just like other things in God's Word that we let fall by the wayside, it has power to change our entire life circumstances.

Here's another layer that's hard to unpack, so let's look at this one slowly: When you come to Jesus "just as you are," let me be clear, the Bible does say that's enough to see your sins forgiven, remembered no more, as far as the east is from the west.[42] But He also offers you a hand up to more. "More" is not required to receive forgiveness, but avoiding the steps that come with confession and service buries a great treasure.

The difference between "covered in forgiveness" and "fully healed" can be found in the lost art of confession—a spiritual practice that can be a gift of release and divine calling for all Christians.

I can only be this sure because I've lived through this process of healing and discovery myself—both the simple and the scary side of it. As

40. Code of Canon Law, Book IV, 988 §1.
41. James 5:16 KJV.
42. See Psalm 103:12.

you know by now, I had a good amount of "scary" to confess, and good reason to be a little worried about the reaction to what I had to share.

Plus, my confession story, though it was facilitated by a priest, happened in public in front of a few of my closest friends in an environment where public image was everything. This was a worst-case scenario for opening my mouth. But God had plans, and when His plans are catching fire, you can't stand still. You can't stare into the burning bush and not turn to face your Pharaoh.

By the time God lights this fire, your only choice is to respond or give up and let it consume you. Let me tell you—you want to respond. He has an exodus from slavery waiting for you. It might take a few rounds of "plaguing" experiences to break free, you might go through some things in your life dying off, and you might find yourself running in circles in a wilderness, wondering if you made the right decision. But He promises to meet you at each of these turns if you keep moving forward. He will split seas and bury enemy pursuits. He will provide for your needs like manna falling from heaven. He will water you from nothing if you stand on the solid rock of His name. All you have to do is go—follow as His spirit leads a pillar of cloud by day, fire by night. He promises to walk you through this in a big way as long as you're walking it out.

So here we go. Walk with me through the most mortifyingly humiliating and ultimately freeing, equipping single night of my entire life. I thought I would die of embarrassment. Instead, I learned to live.

By now you have a picture of my picture-perfect life on the North Shore of Chicago, existing as a totally superficial semblance of myself, living on the surface, polishing anything real and painting over flaws I thought couldn't be seen if I presented myself well enough. I was an area pastor, on stage, often leading groups and teaching men and women—teaching out of my blind spots. I was intimately trying to help people get to their next level of freedom and get real, while I was avoiding my reality—unknowingly, I might add.

I had two children, was pregnant with my third, and had just been diagnosed with placenta previa. I was masking the seriousness of this condition even to myself. In a single thought I could think about how this was life threatening and then dismiss it as nothing to worry about at all. Of course, I'd be fine! Mostly I kept going like it wasn't there. The truth was, at any moment as my pregnancy continued, my baby and I could've bled out and died. My doctors had recommended that I go on complete bedrest for the remainder of my pregnancy. I was compartmentalizing—aware of the threat, but thinking I had to keep life working the same as before, no change, keep up, don't let on. *It'll be fine.*

I'm realizing even now in this moment the similarities between the tangible elements of this health struggle and how I was handling my equally compromised spiritual health—how many of us avoid the realities of compromised spiritual health and "just keep going," knowing we could spiritually bleed out and die, but we do nothing about it. *It'll be fine.*

There is One who literally bled out and died for our sake. He calls us through that act to get real, to come to the foot of that cross where He died and get as honest as the criminal next to Him who spent the last moments of his life rediscovering *the lost art of confession.*[43]

I had a friend at this time who had been magnificently healed of cancer. She was a well-known reporter, so she was the breadwinner, and she heard this priest had a gift for healing. She called me, as her "spiritual friend," to see what I thought. I wasn't sure what to think. I told her, "I'm not Catholic." I grew up with a Pentecostal background, but I was full of judgments. I believed in God's power to heal, though, and I was curious to see her story unfold.

I told her that, as I had seen it, God does have the power to heal; I had just never seen it in a Catholic priest. But she had nothing to lose. My response was, "Go for it!"

---

43. See Luke 23:32–55.

It turned out she had a life-changing experience, received a complete healing, and it rocked her world. She told me after the fact, and with the lingering rush of transformation, she said, "He's coming to my house. Do you want to come?"

Remember, I was dealing with a condition that was life-threatening for me and my unborn baby, but as a total skeptic, I also wasn't going to let anyone know this. If "this guy" and his gift were "for real," then he should be able to hear anything God wanted to say. I wasn't going to make it easy. (Did I mention I was judgy? A lot has changed.)

In line with the life I was living, this was a high-end gathering, driveway filled with Mercedes, the house was packed, and the priest wasted no time. We had just arrived, and he was at the foot of a huge flight of stairs. He said, "Who am I praying with first?" Without hesitation I said, "Me," and raised my hand, but I clearly hadn't thought this through.

I had a girlfriend who had come with me, and my other friend was the host, and the priest asked if I wanted them to come along. What was I going to say in this scenario—in the host's home at the foot of her stairs? No? These were my church friends in a culture of "perfect friends, perfect lives." They had no idea what was under the hood. If I was going to take this seriously—if this was going to work—we were in it together!

We got settled in a room upstairs, and the priest asked me what I wanted prayer for, and I answered, "For the healthy delivery of my baby." I thought I'd gotten away with choosing my words carefully, but he said with the first hint of discernment, "Are you sure? Is that it?" I'd already started out withholding a piece of myself from the process. This was never going to work if I wasn't willing to be truthful. Keep that in mind as you measure your own deep dive into Real Talk. It'll take great effort. It offers great rewards.

I started out lying, he started praying, and the two don't go well together, so it wasn't long before he said, "Something's blocking the prayer, and I can't keep going." He asked if there was another baby, a loss, and some unresolved anger or unforgiveness in my life. He had my attention, but like I've said, I wasn't consciously aware that all my secrets were even secrets. I knew I had lived through personal trauma of all sorts, and that I was living an inauthentic life now, but I didn't see these things as needing to be confessed. So, I answered his question more literally with the first thing that came to mind.

"No, I have two perfect children. No miscarriages. I'm not mad at God."

He continued, though, insistent that what was blocking his prayers was unforgiveness, either toward myself or concerning some leftover anger at God around a baby. He kept with the narrative, saying, " I feel like it involves another baby." That's when the younger priest who was with him said, "Father, I'm feeling it's more of a sin."

It was as if a portal opened. This was 2003. I was thirty-four at the time, and it came to me at once as if it had been waiting for discovery for ages. It hit me eagerly and urgently. I'd had an abortion seventeen years before, when I was seventeen. I had almost forgotten about it; repressed it. He asked if I had ever confessed it. "No, of course not," I replied, stunned. "I'm not Catholic. We don't do confession." I was a Protestant with a master's in clinical psychology, and that was my response. He lovingly laughed and asked if I believed in the Bible and what James 5:16 says:

*Therefore confess your sins to each other and pray for each other so that you may be healed. The prayer of a righteous person is powerful and effective.*

He asked me in so many words, and through His Word, "Would you like to confess this sin and have it removed as far as the east is from the west? To have all that is scarlet returned to the pure white of snow?" I needed a moment (a big moment), to be honest—with God, with myself, and with them if I was willing to experience what comes from true confession, total repentance, **soul healing.** I said *yes!*

The priest began to pray again. He asked if he could anoint me with oil; he began to speak in tongues. I mentioned being surprised, thinking that wasn't a part of his denominational theology, and he laughed. "You've never met a completed Catholic."

He also said, delivering to me the words and wish of Jesus, "Your sins are removed 'as far as the east is from the west,'[44] though they were as scarlet, pure as the driven snow."[45]

It was a short honeymoon of spiritual euphoria and deliverance before he said, "Okay, now I'm hearing that Jesus wants you to do penance." I told him, only half joking, "Father, once again, I'm not Catholic."

Good-humored, he replied, "You Protestants. You have kept a secret for seventeen years—almost two decades. Do you think you might need a little healing to walk this out? Penance is simply steps to walk out your healing."

We all have **soul patterns** of the secrets we have in place, so walking it out is going to travel a different pathway for each person. He suggested lightly, "I feel like Jesus would have you serve in a pro-life center where you can help other girls not to make the same choice."

It was a lot to take in at once. I was still processing the memory, the prayer, the fact that I'd admitted this in front of friends and might have just changed our relationship. I was still reeling from revisiting the memory of the abortion and all the secrets that had led up to that place, which I had completely blocked out. I had been so abused and used by the time I got to the point of having an abortion that I was already a shell of a human being. I was broken, calling out to God, but numb. I was revisiting all of these **soul wounds,** and he wanted me to decide to serve others in the space of my greatest darkness?

I literally had a "come to Jesus" moment, and I contemplated deeply before, fully resigned, I said yes.

---

44. Psalm 103:12.
45. Isaiah 1:18: "Though your sins are like scarlet, they shall be as white as snow; though they are red as crimson, they shall be like wool."

But we still weren't done. Unbelievably, we were just getting started! "The Lord is telling me you have a few more open doors," he said.

"You've got to be kidding me—no more open doors, please," I thought to myself. "I'm sitting here before my two beautiful, perfect friends, who live in their beautiful, perfect homes with our seemingly beautiful, perfect lives, and here mine is, being unpackaged with a sledgehammer."

Here we go—let's kick down doors number two through eternity— sins, secrets, and shame. This would be the definition of spilling my actual guts, and it felt just about how you'd expect.

You've already heard the bulk of it in the last chapter. Sexual abuse, more than once, with more than one person I knew. Repeating sexual behaviors inappropriately as a kid. Equating acceptance with sexual attention because of my circumstances. I numbed through alcohol abuse at a young age, and I had never talked about this numbing or all the things I'd done to survive.

There were other things I didn't even mention—the occultic effects of things that were commonplace in my childhood, especially in my family's culture, engaging with horoscopes "religiously," and turning to Tarot cards, seances, or Ouija for fun. I never thought these had any effect, but the priest brought them up as legitimate open doors to the occult. Add the teen and adult years—struggles with pornography brought fully in unity into my marriage, psychology as idolatry, a multitude of abusive behaviors. The younger priest who had called out my abortion earlier said, "Wow, Father, that's a lot of sin."

"Let me tell you," I said, not joking at all, "I was raised in the '80s in Fort Lauderdale with family trauma, divorced parents, and the last name Melendez, so yeah, I could tell you stories."

Joking aside, when I started listing things and naming the open doors, he described all of the above as "places you've not let the Lord clear and cover."

I'd come this far. It was all out there now. So, in the words of Simon Peter, "Then, Lord...not just my feet but my hands and my head as well!"[46] I had been trying to cover them myself—covering what wasn't healed, what I didn't want to see, and things I'd never dealt with. That didn't work at all. My God wanted them uncovered so He could cover them with His sufficient grace instead.[47]

A fascinating shift was happening in this moment—and it was just a drop in the bucket compared to the shift that was to come, one that hasn't stopped shifting since, shocking me with His glory and goodness: a formula for eternal purpose.

That's easy to say in hindsight—but in the moment, it was a bit of a horror show. By the time he'd "cleared out all the open doors," I was humiliated, embarrassed, mortified. I wanted to bury my face in the ground because of what people could now see. Including all my mascara running.

But that's the thing. The Lord already sees, and *He* wanted it cleared out.

That's when the willingness in me began to shift from self-focused (self-centered) to moved by His monumental love. It was dawning on me, "How can the Lord love me so much that He would put all these pieces in place to do this?" If He wanted this for me to this degree, there must be not only monumental love—but a monumental reason. Eternally and on earth.

That's where I was emotionally and spiritually—in this mix of mortification and immersive mercy—when the priest said from out of left field, "Now that all of that is out of the way, I can hear the Lord perfectly—and He's talking about the baby."

I had nearly forgotten.

This is what I came for—but I'd been on a whiplash tour through time, multiple lives, and dimensions of trauma, healing, and deliverance.

---

46. John 13:9.
47. See 2 Corinthians 12:9.

"There's something going on with your placenta." He dropped the bomb that dispersed my judgy skepticism, never to retake solid form. It was less of an explosive experience than I would have imagined for a word from God. It was just a supernatural, humbling moment of awe and wonder. So much had transpired, this felt almost expected at this point. Bring it on.

I was mortified though, because now the priest clearly knew I had withheld this from him. I told him I was so sorry I didn't tell him. In return, I received, oh, this beautiful wisdom: "It's okay—He wanted to clear out everything else first because He loves you that much. He tells us to 'confess our sin *that we might be healed.*'" This self-named "completed Catholic" reminded me, "Those things were in the way. You've got to be clean to come to the altar."

"Young lady," he said, "you've received more emotional and spiritual healing than I've ever seen. Believe that the Lord can heal you physically."

"Absolutely. I know He can."

He prayed again, anointed me with oil, and simply said, "You have received a complete healing. (Don't resume regular activity until you see your doctor.) But you are healed! All is perfectly restored." Then he emphasized, "I don't know who you are or what God is calling you to do, but I've never had a night like tonight." I believe that moment is where the gift of Real Talk began.

There it was. This deliverance meant everything to me, but it wasn't just about me. It was about the others God already had a plan to reach and to release just as powerfully—an endless stream of letting go and living free.

"God has one more gift for you," he said, and I thought, "No, really, that's okay. I'm good."

"He wants to give you the gift of tears."

I felt a cutting loose, not sure I could possibly receive more, yet fearful and excited at the same time.

"You've had to harden your heart to get through all you had to get through. He wants to restore in you a heart of flesh."

Waterfalls. The tears came without measure. Dramatic crying. I began smelling incense with no idea what it was. I would later be told it was the manifestation of the scent of what the priests would burn when they entered the holy of holies with a sin offering.

The deepest core of my life's missional purpose came next. I was told, "There is an ecumenical anointing on your life to bring unity to churches." God used two streams I had been wounded in—Pentecostal and Catholic—to bring me healing through a charismatic Catholic priest. I don't believe I could have reconciled those two areas if God had not packaged them exactly as He did.

If I hadn't gone through this healing, I wouldn't know. I wouldn't have sought out this work or found this path. Confession—walking it out—speaking up about the unspeakable things in order to disarm their power to hold us back, so that others can find release through our example—the healing that comes through this process is important *because* the pathways you walk out as a result are eternally imperative.

I knew I needed to act quickly on the "penance" I wasn't sure about ("I'm not Catholic."). The next morning, I opened the Yellow Pages. (Remember those? It's Google on paper. Yellow paper.) I figured I could make the effort by calling and leaving a message. My plan was to ask, "Do you need any volunteers? I have my master's in clinical psychology, and I used to be pro-choice, but I guess I am now pro-life." I didn't know much more after that. Unfortunately, they answered the phone and seemed to already know what I needed. They invited me in the next day, and that began my journey to true reconciliation, deep healing, and walking it out. I took the first step, and God has been directing me ever since. We just need to say yes, and He will usher us in. He has storerooms, untapped.

Here I was, the penitent Protestant, volunteering in a pro-life clinic when I used to be pro-choice. I didn't know how this was supposed to help or what was happening to me, but I'd had an experience, and the Lord was so complete in what He worked in me that I wanted to finish what He started, whatever it was. I wanted it all. At this point, I was honestly scared not to be obedient.

God also knew that an area I needed to work on was this area of judginess I mentioned. I needed to let go of something I refer to as "never vows." Things we say we'd "never do" or that we'd "never be like," "never struggle with," things we can "never understand" someone else doing.

There's a reason for the phrase "never say never." God hears our cocky assurance and says, "Really? Let's see about that." Then the cock crows three times.[48] The enemy hears you swear, "I would never," and says, "Oh really? Let me surprise you with your vast capacity for failure and make you doubt God could love someone as weak as you."

There's a bigger reason too: these never-vows are judgments where we fall short of entering into a place of healing love for others. We eliminate our ability to walk out our healing—and to walk others toward theirs—if we don't find this place of seeing them from God's perspective and serving them in their spiritual need boldly but without judgment.

That's when the confession journey began to multiply. I saw the power of paying the encounter forward. As I shifted, I met different kinds of shift on every corner:

Your first confession is for your healing. When someone else hears your confession as it becomes your confessed testimony, they say time and time again, "I thought I was the only one."

You can have an encounter, but if you don't walk it out, it doesn't work. That's why we built Real Talk the way we did. We start with a healing encounter, but you need to walk it out if you're going to have lasting results. If you don't stick around to let the Lord rebuild spiritual muscle you've lost over time, you don't get to experience a changed pathway or affect others with your life change.

---

48. See Matthew 26:31–35.

We can't impact others until we've been impacted ourselves first—confessed, healed, made new. It's true of individuals, of relationships, raising children, even the cultural development of civilizations throughout history. It's true of our global church. How can we be the refuge—the beacon of healing and harbor we're meant to be—if we ourselves are unhealed and unwilling to hear? Unwilling to hear the need for us to change. Unwilling to hear of others' sin, pain, and struggle with compassion for their healing. We tell our children we cannot be good leaders until we learn to be followers, but we are unwilling to follow when it comes to the hard work of developing our own humbled, healed hearts.

In the midst of my confession experience, there was pain in revisiting painful memories. Yet without that excavation, something can have a hold on you and succeed lifelong in holding you back or holding you down. It's the enemy's greatest joy: holding you back from purpose, holding you down from the joy of the Lord in which you are already free to live—if you are willing. Going *through* the pain, the excavation, the confession, the Red Sea of your fears and unbelief—going through it moves you dynamically forward toward a promised purpose God has clearly mapped out for you. Going forward moves you off the treadmill and onto the threshold of complete life change.

We *need* to talk—to confess—to walk it out. Otherwise, an encounter is just an exercise in vanity. We need to excavate the deepest corners with God and with trusted people we can surround ourselves with, and we need to explore where we need to cut strings, forgive ourselves, and receive God's forgiveness completely, which also frees us to forgive others who have been a part of these debilitating pieces of our past.

The healing isn't complete—isn't fulfilled by living in our purpose—until we tell the story, or until we learn a whole new way of living where confession and transparency are at the center. There's hardly a room I walk into nowadays that I don't start sharing boldly and comfortably some part of my story that I used to keep hidden. I'm no longer afraid of it—which is so freeing and powerful to be able to say. But there's way more than that: I've seen too many times—Too. Many. Times.—the power that confession has on others. It's the most inspiring and encouraging ripple effect of God's heart you'll ever witness.

I dare you to try it. I dare you to seek out confession and the spiritual impact of the stories we tell. It's a lost art.

We all have a tale to tell and an eternal, imperative reason to tell it. You likely know what yours is. The question is, are you ready for how God wants to use you through it?

If you are…let's keep going.

# CHAPTER 6

# SPEAK THE UNSPEAKABLE

Things that we keep inside become shades of gray that lead to
darker places, and things that we let out are shades of light that
lead to freedom.

Secrets were unearthed. My "confession" was the first time I'd spoken
any of those unspeakable things out loud, but it wouldn't be the last.
What I didn't know was the power that doing so would have in my own
life and a world of others. Speaking the Unspeakable (and its related
spiritual impact) would become my life's work and eternal purpose.

Every day. I tell you, I see some piece of it every day. In small groups
that I work with, going through Real Talk committed to one another
in confidentiality. In church leadership teams where we're resetting the
culture of the church from the inside out. In boardrooms, television stu-
dios, and parliamentary podiums. In any of these settings, the common
denominator I see is in the eyes of someone God loves being set free.

Each time, you can feel it before it happens. When truth is shared,
and a toe dipped into Real Talk, the room begins to shift, tears well, and
hurting hearts respond, "I thought I was the only one."

You never are. You never will be. The war we wage is common to all. You've heard this by now for several chapters—how you're not alone and how the whisper of secrets set free is not so quietly transforming churches, business, families, and communities—rumbling under the continents and shifting the very foundation of God's church on earth.

What we're unpacking here is the "why" that reaches beyond you. The Real Talk process that invites people to speak the unspeakable, to give light to the unspoken, is a call to freedom where everyone—men, women, children, leaders, teachers, friends, and loved ones—begins to speak up and say, "Us too."

This is where understanding takes root and the real work begins. We're inching toward the place where you adopt your own passion for speaking the unspoken, as you're given the tools and permission (often for the first time in your life) to say what you've never said.

We've spent our time together processing your need for and invitation to total personal transformation.

*NOW WE'RE ON THE PRECIPICE OF ACTION, WHERE WE SHIFT FROM BEING ALL TALK (PUN INTENDED) TO GETTING REAL. THE JOURNEY TO MORE BEGINS HERE.*

We also shift here from external observation (what's wrong, what's needed) to the internal, accepting that this is us and deciding that we're going to work the steps, so to speak.

It's already happening beyond us. The question is if we're going to be a part of that change or stay in the silent, heavy, shackled past. The world of silence where we've been living is starting to shift culturally.

If you're ready to shift personally, then you're ready for your defining moment.

As we begin to dig in here and do the excavating work of self-discovery and revelation, odds are we've hit an aha moment or two, with something you can relate to. Something that reads your mail. Something God is using to make you uncomfortable (not "okay with").Whatever you know you can't stand anymore: your secret, your shame, your addiction (alcohol, pornography, infidelity, domestic violence, abuse)—some are even packaged as good (overworking, serving, striving, running another Iron Man, or never saying no).

*WHATEVER YOU'RE STRUGGLING WITH IS BEING PERPETUATED BY YOUR INABILITY TO TALK ABOUT IT.*

That sounds like we're over simplifying, but we've established, and I'll repeat, that confession (speaking up) and healing are biblical and inextricably tied together. We have a very simple directive from God where promise and provision come from following His Word. Sometimes we don't take biblical instruction seriously or literally, and I encourage you: When we don't, we're missing out.

Here's a little secret to this pivot point we're in: When we learn the value of speaking up, we realize the surprising ease of the habit of it. It's like the adage that practice makes perfect. Or the common principles behind building any habits through regularity, consistency, and repetition. We have become ensconced in a concrete encasement of silence. It's a safe familiarity and coping mechanism most of us have had in place forever.

Habits of silence can also sometimes come from well-intentioned places of discipline, respect, and self-control. Children are seen and not heard. (That's actually a horrible starting ground—we need kids to speak up!) Friends are drama-free, being the "bigger man" and turning a cheek. Good employees keep their head down and do the work. So, if it ain't broke, why fix it? Because unless it's out of the right heart, these are ways to stay invisible and endure. But false peace isn't peace at all.

Because it *is* broken in the broader sense, and it's breaking us, our relationships, our systems, our communities, and our hearts. It's breaking our bond of greater potential in God and what He'd like to do in our lives if we were brave enough to do it His way.

Here's the good news about that: If it's habit that got us here, then it's habit that will get us out, and a simple shift in habit is not insurmountable; it's surprisingly accessible.

We're used to keeping things hidden, our cards close to our vest, hoping others won't catch on to our imperfections. We're convinced revelation would be taking off our Kardashian mask and being shunned for the mess of imperfection and sin we are underneath. But when we try it—when we say, "This is who I am, this is what I struggle with, what I need help with; this is what I've survived and what God walked me through and can walk you through too," and we feel and see the difference—relief, deliverance, launching into purpose—we get a taste of something. After that taste, it's so easy to want more. You will find yourself asking why you didn't try this earlier.

It's not your fault—it does look scary, and no one is teaching this. Not our churches, not our families, for the most part, and certainly not our human nature. It goes against every instinct we have. But the thing it does not go against is the Word, and the Word works.

Not only are we entrenched in habits of silence, hiding, faking, and straight lying, but the sins and imperfections that we try to hide are usually habits themselves, with deeply rooted reasons and sources.

Sometimes your secret is linked to habits you formed as a kid and your feeling that you aren't good enough or your fear of being rejected or never fitting in. Then as an adult, for similar reasons of seeking belonging and security of acceptance, you need a hit from the fillers you believe make you feel better.

How did you build that emotional point of reference? When something happens and you meet it with compromise, indulgence, giving-in, handling situations with your own broken tools instead of the Lord's, it opens a door to either opportunity or escape. It either feels good (emotionally, physically, mentally) or it keeps you from something that doesn't feel good—it gets you what you (think you) want or helps you avoid what you don't want. This is a tricky trade, though, because the Word makes it clear the "heart is deceitful above all things,"[49] and as Paul writes, "What I want to do I do not do, but what I hate I do."[50] Simply, what we want is not always to be trusted and can be a terrible informer of God's best for us.

In this pattern of being human and making "felt" decisions, you let something happen, or make it happen, and you don't really label it. You don't name it, especially because no one is helping you name it, so it just gets normalized. Habitualized. You identify it (perhaps subconsciously) as acceptable, survivable, and "just the way I am," or "the way life goes."

No. And no again. Sometimes it's as simple as deciding or realizing these ways are not the way it is or has to be, and calling them what they are instead, which is anything from a shortcut to a millstone around your neck.[51]

When we've normalized a want, a behavior, a pattern, it puts a nice shiny bumper sticker on your forehead, and you begin to put out this spiritual frequency that "I'm okay with this," so then you attract everything of that frequency.

49. Jeremiah 17:9.
50. Romans 7:15.
51. See Matthew 18:6.

Most of the things that trip us up are embedded in our personal history, which includes our individual track record of choices and childhood and our "nature and nurture" that draws heavily from the habits and histories of those around us.

How did it get that way? Not speaking about it.

(The grooming was undetected; it was normalized.)

How does it change? Speaking about it.

(Realizing you are no longer in agreement with the narrative and want to "un"-normalize it.)

No matter how unspeakable your "it" may seem.

We've said this in a few ways, and we'll say it again: Awareness is the first step, then comes courage. Speaking up can be victoriously disarming. With few exceptions, when we speak of unspeakable things, we often discover they weren't "unspeakable" after all. You are able to tell them. They might feel unspeakable, as in harmful, hard to endure, hard to face, but they are "speakable." When you are able to confess and bring up your secrets, it brings you out of your false prison into a healing space. Speaking up often robs unspeakable things of their fangs and turns their menacing roar into a defeated whimper.

There's a theory in art, especially filmmaking, that the more a thing is unseen, the more frightening it can be or more threatening its power. Your imagination fills in the blanks and multiplies the threat that exists in reality. There's always a bogeyman in the closet or under the bed—until you turn on the lights.

It doesn't matter where you are in your life, personal or spiritual development, or current situation, taking a Real Talk approach is just as transformative under any circumstances. Not to downplay the seriousness and urgency, but it is truly one size fits all.

That's part of the testimony you can lean into for your own sense of security when taking this leap. We have adapted this tool for all grades and for leadership—a way to take back the narrative with authority. God's Word is a blanket that covers all in the same standard of truth and promise, and this work is nothing if it is not built on, made of, and totally dependent on the biblical principles He's laid out.

One of our Real Talk participants referenced her age specifically during the first leaders meeting. In her newfound hunger to "finally" name things, she said, "I'm seventy-four, and this conversation is making me realize for the first time that something happened to me when I was little. I'm tired of pretending it didn't happen, I want to talk about it, and I want to understand why it happened!" People are starving in the church to let openness be normalized instead of all the hiding. Instead of allowing sin, shame, hurt, and betrayal to hold you back, just say all the crazy things you've never had a place to say.

If church isn't that place, where is? If not at the foot of the cross or sitting at the feet of Jesus as Rabbi and friend, your other option is the world. The world will let you say anything. Then it will tear you apart and leave you behind. The prince of darkness, and of this world, offers a very fake and temporary invitation while the church has told us to stay silent. Don't ask, don't tell. Don't let on. Act Christian. But we don't even know what it means anymore to act Christian.

What it really looks like is surprising to most. It looks like someone able to confess that, "I do the thing I don't want to do."[52] It means admitting, "I am sick of this part of myself." It means being honest about who we were and how we were living and honestly accepting we were truly made for more.

This isn't just an idea—this is a process that's currently being put into practice for growing numbers of people, institutions, and organizations around the world. The rubber has already hit the road, and on the way, there isn't one who hasn't told a resulting story of victory.

---

52. See Romans 7:15: "I do not understand what I do. For what I want to do I do not do, but what I hate I do."

We had an older gentleman who admitted, "I've had a gambling addiction as long as I can remember that was gone—*gone*—after I was simply able to talk about it *because the feeling of shame and hiding was perpetuating my addiction.* I was able to unpack and heal things that I couldn't talk about that were the root that had actually caused my addiction. It was never about gambling; there was something behind it. I was able to cut a cord that had been holding me down my whole life."

Don't miss this equation.

The visible issue was gambling, and it seemed insurmountable when what he was fighting is just what you see—addiction. But that's just the symptom. There's no power in simply "never placing that bet again." Short of a supernatural healing, which is possible, the ability to suddenly avoid a habitual sin on basic willpower is, simply put, a bad bet.

Gambling isn't the thing. No vice is the thing. It's the effect of that vice—relief, escape, numbing, acceptance, security, personal gain, self-destruction—that we're after. The impact is our drug, an almost medicinal sensation that seems to alleviate our pain for a short time. If we can figure out why we need that numbing—what we're trying to fill, escape, or cure—we're more equipped in that battle than simply avoiding a well-armed, massively magnetic vice.

Talking about it does several things at once: It disarms one of the strongest hands that holds us down—shame, fear, embarrassment, risk of exposure. It teaches us these things are not as frightening as they seem. It turns us to an understanding of the "real" struggle, the source of the problem that leads us to our destructive habits, and it gives us the tools to fight those battles and win. The key to accessing the whole process is talking about it. Speaking what you thought was unspeakable.

*A TURN OF PHRASE.*
*A TURN OF THE KEY.*
*A TURN OF A CORNER.*
*A TURNING AROUND.*

There was another woman whose story was desperately in need of Real Talk. She was drowning in the world of sex trafficking. She was abused in her youth (by a family member), and her mother knew about it, which is all too common a story. Her pastor grandfather just thought she was becoming troubled. Generational inability to see and speak what everyone is more comfortable hiding is rampant. She found "refuge" in her teenage boyfriend who ended up grooming her to be trafficked. She ended up on drugs and had a baby used as leverage to keep her in trafficking. It was mess upon mess, shame upon shame. She was in and out of rehab more than twenty times.

*SHE DIDN'T HAVE A DRUG PROBLEM;*
*SHE HAD A SHAME PROBLEM.*

She was trying to escape from or mask the shame that she couldn't tell anyone about, and therefore she couldn't turn from the very thing pushing her inevitably to medicate and numb the shame. The alternative—the need here—is to be delivered from that shame and told with authority, "That is not who you are. Whatever has been done to you and what you have done is not you." That is the only trustworthy first step to not needing to be medicated anymore. That's how you fight it. That's how you disarm. That's how you break free.

Like the other gentleman's issue with gambling or any of the other stories:

> *YOU'RE POWERLESS TO FIGHT THE VISIBLE ISSUE IF YOU DON'T UNDERSTAND THE INVISIBLE BATTLE.*

When she finally got to talk about her story and grieve all that was stolen and the fact that she never had an advocate, she was able to withdraw from long-term drug use (no easy task)—not because she had solved her drug problem through sobriety, but because no one had ever told her the things we're talking about here. No one ever gave her permission and a safe space to talk freely, unedited, and without judgment about all that had happened, and be set free from it, accepted, loved, and redirected. No one got down to the root and drilled down to how or why all this happened.

Once she started talking about all the ways she'd been used for sex—the first time it happened, how it felt to have her mother not advocate for her, how she was viewed as stupid at school (when in fact she wasn't stupid—rather, she was traumatized and couldn't focus, thinking about what would happen again and again), how it felt when she was forced into situations by people she trusted and then arrested because she was seen as a "prostitute." To sit at church and be seen as a church youth leader one day and be shunned the next. When she was able to grieve, she was able to remove the labels and see she was so much more.

She wasn't stupid. She wasn't cheap. *And there is no such thing* as a child-prostitute. She was trying to find love, trusting authority figures, learning falsely that love blended with abuse, confused by trust being rewritten as a child until she couldn't see that being sold was not who she was.

We say in the organization, and I've told my kids, especially my boys, there's no such thing as a prostitute. The word is off the table. You never use it, and if you hear it, you correct it out there in the world. I tell them: "If you ever hear someone use the term *hooker* or *prostitute*, what do you say?" They reply with a bit of an eyeroll due to repetition and "mom" voice, "We know, Mom—that's a girl with a story." I don't mind the eyeroll. What matters is, they've learned,

*SHE'S A GIRL WITH A STORY, WHO NEVER HAD A PLACE TO TELL IT OR SOMEONE TO RESCUE HER...YET!*

Same for anyone under any disparaging label or diagnosis we like to slap onto things because it's easy, dismissive, and makes us feel better about ourselves and our perceived social order. But all of us are a girl, a guy, a person with a story who never had a place to tell it. We've never been ushered to a true offramp.

You do, though, have a place, if we create it—if we begin living as the church He created us to be, both in our personal temples and lives and in the places of worship we call His house. If you take that opportunity for yourself, you build that opportunity for others through telling your story and giving others the permission to tell theirs—*all* of it. You're turning the whole ship in the water.

Nowhere is this more needed than in church, and especially in the church in America where we've become so whitewashed and watered down. Anyone walks through the front door with a label, an image, a problem we think we've defined as going against God, we relegate them, isolate them, judge them, and frown upon them, and we think that's being Christlike—upholding the standard.

First of all, if we measure His actual standard, none of us are upholding it ourselves anyway, just in less "defined" and socially outcast ways. But let's be honest—coveting made His top-10 hit list of sins that separate us from being holy and deserving redemption, and most of us practice that sin in small ways daily. Thankfully, nothing can separate us from His love,[53] no matter how hard we and the enemy both work at it. And Christ in His perfection closes that gap to come to us.

Second, upholding His standard *means* going to the most broken among us with a mending hand of perfect love. There are several women labelled as "prostitutes" who play key roles in the gospel story, but there are zero perfectly faithful followers ("Christians") who do. Talk about a girl with a story—these were girls with gospel stories that would lead to the living, breathing legacy of Christ on earth.

(It should be noted these were stories of redemption and not "leaving things as they were." Where their stories encountered the true power of God, they chose faith.)

Rahab, part of the lineage that led to the birth of Christ, showed faith in action during a pivotal moment of protecting others. Mary Magdalene became the inadvertent example that showed the disciples what sincere, sacrificial worship looked like as she gave "a year's wages worth"[54] for a moment of elevating Jesus. She sat at the literal feet of Jesus. And the cross. And the grave. She showed up, and hers was the first name Jesus spoke in His resurrection. Why? Why does God choose this story out of any way this could have been lived and written?

---

53. See Romans 8:31–39.
54. John 12:5 NLT: "That perfume was worth a year's wages. It should have been sold and the money given to the poor."

*BECAUSE HE'S CALLING YOUR NAME*
*JUST THE SAME.*

Mary is one of your many inarguable, biblical examples that it's not about what we've done to deserve it. His resurrection, not your unspeakable path, brings Him to a place of calling out your name.

The world cast Mary out. The disciples cast her down, deemed her less worthy of Jesus than they, and scorned her for making "wasteful" decisions about extravagant worship. That extravagant worship took her to the cross—took her to the tomb—and put her in a place where, when she heard the call of her name, she recognized the One who spoke and responded.

*SHE WAS JUST A GIRL WITH A STORY. WHEN*
*SHE WALKED WITH JESUS, SHE HAD A PLACE*
*TO TELL IT AND TO BE REDEEMED.*

Jesus creates that place to be outspoken about our story and His. To speak the unspeakable and make a place where others can speak out as well. To go and tell the nations what could happen next if we answer when He calls.

This is what I learned—to confess, to speak, to make a place for others—and now, this is where I live. It's what I do with my life and what we do in the Real Talk program. Wherever and whoever you are, whatever you're facing, Real Talk normalizes the ability to say whatever you need to say to start unburdening left and right, and from the inside out—way out, as your bravery begets bravery and this work ripples out (more on this when we learn how *when we shift, everything shifts*).

It may not be easy, depending on your story. But that's all right too, because without a doubt, **you were born to battle...**

# PART 3:

# REFLECT

# CHAPTER 7

# BORN TO BATTLE

The minute you are created, person meets purpose, and that's
when the battle begins. The enemy wants to separate us from
our purpose. Thankfully, you were born to battle.

People, get ready. This is where the hardest work begins. This is the
"your mission if you choose to accept it" point of your journey that
sets the pace for the rest of the process. This is where you move from
bystander to a place of personal calling and setting out on the road
toward fulfilling it.

Fair warning, the battle isn't easy. I get it. I know from personal
experience. It wears you down. It's *exhausting*. In contrast, it's *exhilarating*
to step into a battle you were created to win. As sons and daughters,
we've been knighted for this. It's not for the faint of heart, but there are
ways you can become more bulletproof.

The Bible makes it clear that:

Before you were even "knit together in your mother's womb," you
were known.[55]

---

55. See Psalm 139:13–14.

As long as you've been known, you've had a known purpose.[56]

As long as you've had a purpose, the battle has been on to bring you down.[57]

But God...has already factored that in and provides the way to win.[58]

It's a law of spiritual nature. The enemy wants to separate you from your purpose. The minute you're born, he's doing this. He's coming at us from the word "go," and *he's never going to drop his purpose until he's stolen yours.*

For most of us—our eyes aren't even open to the battle. None of us fully know the degree of the war being waged for our soul and our thwarted purpose to be a force for eternal good. We've barely breathed our first sip of earthly air, and Satan is already working the long game. By the time we're old enough to get involved, we're not close to matching his marathon. We're not even keeping pace with a spiritual sprint. Honestly, we don't even know we're in a race.

This isn't meant to discourage you, and it *shouldn't*. Instead, this is your aha moment where you unearth the enemy's well-hidden plan and pick up the hope that if you know about his playbook, you have the advantage. *Understanding the attack defines your defense*, and you can "gird up" and be ready instead of caught unaware and overwhelmed. This is where you get the tools and the takeaway that gets you an upper hand in this fight.

Let me stress, yes, God has already won the victory over the end of your story, but some feel blocked from embracing that victory for themselves. Others are having their day-to-day victory stolen or have "lost signal" in trying to connect to a sense of purpose and identity. When we say throughout this book that you were made for more, that includes the fact that you were made for this—no matter what your "this" is.

---

56. See Jeremiah 1:5.
57. See Ephesians 6:12.
58. See Philippians 1:6.

How can you be sure? Because it's all the same tired, predictable formula from the enemy. He is not original, and he is always repetitive. It's almost confusing and definitely embarrassing how the same tactics work on us human beings that have been working from the beginning. Fear, jealousy, want, a hunger for love and acceptance. Cain killed Abel out of shame and want of acceptance. The wealthy man in the parable walked away from Christ "very sad" because he knew he was choosing the temporal over the eternal but couldn't get past the insecurity and fear of losing earthly riches.[59] Peter denied Christ publicly in a pivotal moment out of fear of retribution and people's reaction to his faith. He regretted it immediately and broke his own heart, but the devil had gotten a foothold.[60]

Satan knows our weaknesses as human beings with a predictable human nature. He doesn't stop there, though. He studies our individual proclivities, our tender points, and our Achilles heels. He knows exactly where to aim the arrow for a direct and weakening hit. He knows the wounds of our childhood and past. He knows our fears and where our skin is thin, where we're worn down. He knows your vulnerabilities and keeps hitting you, creating this gaping spiritual stab wound that keeps opening, keeps that issue "unclosed," so you have no chance to heal. Eventually you begin to believe you are *unable* to be healed. That's what he does. That's how he wins. He can kill your spirit while you still live.

## THE INCUBATOR OF THE SOUL

My open wounds were attacked by circumstances again and again, perfectly setting me up to die inside. Arrow after arrow came flying: my sister being killed, my dad leaving, my mom sharing too much for a child's understanding about why he was leaving, my brother joining the Navy and leaving at a vulnerable time, and my being abused,

59. See Mark 10:22.
60. See Ephesians 4:27: "And do not give the devil a foothold."

being raped, turning to promiscuity and alcohol to convince myself it was normal and to numb the pain, and having an abortion to hide even more. I couldn't heal from any of it as new wounds kept tearing me apart and nobody was paying attention; no one knew how to talk about it. I didn't know the battle had a purpose of its own.

When my sister was killed, I was young, and I lost my only healthy relational connection. She was erased, and I was left with a very efficient mom who cooked and cleaned like nobody's business but was stoic by nature and didn't do the emotional thing—my emotions were seen as a weakness, and I had no positive example to follow. My dad was busy and living out his Latin roots, and my brother was gone. My chaotic, loud home suddenly grew silent.

As all my other family was grieving, I was left as the youngest hiding silently among all the reeling, tragic death. I was the least significant part of the equation. My grief didn't matter. My role was to be intuitive and quiet and learn how to make everyone else feel better if I wanted a comforting environment for myself.

Already bleeding from these events, I was abused in the happiest place of my childhood. I lived for summer getaways in Arkansas and the surrounding joy of church families. At home, in the Baptist church, I had all the Awana accolades: Chum of the Year, Girl Leader of the Year, fastest at all the Sword Drills. The Pentecostal Holiness Church was my getaway filled with gospel music. I loved the charismatic expression that was so fun and different when I was away from home. I was building a genuine love for God. Right there, in that incubator of my soul, is where I was abused by a family friend who was inextricable from any of those environments and even tied to the music as a worship leader.

## SUPERHEROES ARE TARGETS

If someone had told me, "Hey, there are going to be things that come against you to try to steal, kill, and destroy you—kill what you were made for," I could have seen these things for what they were and surmounted them. I could have identified them in the moment, instead of thinking I was not worth any good, forgotten by God or hated. I would have been better equipped to see this attack for what it was and ask God to pull me through it to my purpose. If I'd been given the tools to talk about it, I could have changed environments earlier and stopped other ripple effects of damage. I'm grateful to have ever found out, though, because so many never do.

I can tell you that now I know: I was made to guard and advocate for the church. That's my passion and my eternal purpose. I have been made sure of that. So of course things came at me trying to kill me and keep me from caring or carrying a sword in the battle.

All the choices I made that aided the enemy in my destruction, as we've already hit on, were symptoms of a bigger illness. I was raised as "super church girl," and I was raped, had sex, had an abortion. None of it was talked about, so none of it was explained or healed. Why? Because there was no place where or person to whom (I thought) I could confess it that wouldn't lead to deeper shame or judgment and rejection, and that was more than I could handle. I was still in church every week, but I had no offramp, no Real Talk model church to speak of the unspeakable things that had happened and learn how to change my trajectory.

Can you imagine the power if we raised our kids this way? Telling them from Sunday school classes to bedtime prayers, "You're a superhero, and because you have this amazing purpose that was planted in heaven, things are going to come at you just like a superhero. You will be a target. Someone might try to touch you in a way that you don't want and say words about you that are untrue. But it's all a ploy because of how important you are, and the truth is, you are *more than a conquerer*,[61] and we can fight whatever weapon is formed against you

---

61. See Romans 8:37: "No, in all these things we are more than conquerors through him who loved us."

by whatever villain. Even if you mess up all by yourself, you were born to battle, not to be beaten down, and we can work to get you back on track."

This is missing from any environment where kids' hopes and habits are forming. Most of us don't know how to do this in our homes, no matter how strong our faith, and it's certainly not happening in our churches and schools. Teachers tend to like the performers, and kids who have some sort of personal conflict going on are the ones who typically don't perform, so no one advocates on their behalf. A high percentage of the time, these are also the exact kids who have a higher calling on their life, by definition of the "bigger battle" that's trying to take them down.

## NOTHING IS UNSPEAKABLE

We were created to be life *givers* and to replicate life—emotionally, spiritually, or physically—which is why the topic of abortion is so central to this battle. We're never going to be victorious about anything if we begin with criticizing a woman who's had an abortion. Almost every woman I've worked with who's had an abortion has been abused in some way at some time. So this isn't a matter of pro-choice or pro-life, it's a conversation about "wounding makes us do things we never thought we'd do," or "wounding has brought me to a place where I don't see the wounds caused by abortion at all."

Hear me: When I'm leading groups for women—high level women in leadership, including church leaders, CEOs, movers and shakers—I hear the stories of woundedness. I've never met a single woman who said she was fulfilled by her freedom to abort, or who didn't express a degree of damage, loss, confusion, and regret.

I teach this in all places, most of all in my home. I tell my kids, "I know who you are and so does God. You are a gift and a light, and you have a calling—and so does any baby you play a role in conceiving. I don't care how it happened, I don't care if you think it's the wrong time or you can't handle it, we'll figure out how to raise him or her because we can't lose this baby's purpose *or yours* to shame and regret." The cycle begins again with that baby—a new life is created, person meets purpose, battle begins.

My kids and their kids and all their fears and perceived mistakes will not have to find their way through the dark of seeking abortions because they're afraid of being found out and believe life would be over if anyone knew. They don't live in past cultures where teens and young adults were sent away to hide in shame in a clandestine "summer vacation with a relative," that was hiding a pregnancy and giving a child away for adoption (nothing wrong with the adoption side but everything's wrong with the shame side for the mother, who is never the same). Whatever happens to my kids, they won't have to figure it out alone, because they know there is nothing—*nothing*—that they cannot come home and say. **NOTHING is unspeakable.** Say all of it out loud so we can take it to God, call it what it is, disarm the enemy, and battle our way through.

## MASTER CURATORS OF STORYTIME

I keep talking about this truth in terms of abortion because that's a piece of my own personal path, but the same "transparent overlay" of grace and truth applies, no matter the battleground you lay it over. It starts as simply as exposing the voices of accusation from an array of sources: relationships that keep us down, pressure from friends, siblings, authority figures, lies and thoughts we come into agreement with internally, the role of marriage when it begins the slow fade to grey and toxic.

There are endless ways that the enemy speaks with the same voice, presented in a different body—the same spirit whose only goal is to keep us living under our purpose. The enemy's foothold digs in deep with the spirit of whatever fear, anxiety, or rejection is plaguing us, speaking our language, and hanging on through generational ties or "sins of the father."[62]

Most heartbreakingly, the church is high on that list of derailing influences, and sometimes it's in first place. I had a pastor who, in his seventies, was moved to tears when he realized he had shut down some of the closest people in his life by not being open to that full conversation that would enable them to name all and allow the past to truly lose its power. After this experience, he declared that he would devote the rest of his life to allowing space for this. The church cannot just feed the hungry and evangelize the lost without also making a pathway for its own to truly lay down their burdens and confess all to work in their full freedom and calling. Without that pathway, we serve, but not to the capacity of who we were born to be. We're locked down, with so much brokenness hidden right beside us.

How do we come back from this when such an insurmountable course correction is needed? How do we get back those who have left (and understandably so, considering how the church has functioned over the last fifty years or more)? Like we've said, the enemy is playing the long game while we're just focused on the weekend. We're not keeping people in faith or keeping them alive. We've gone silent ourselves while other agendas are working to silence us. The enemy doubled down on his plan, and we have no plan to come alongside individual lives to fix this, or a big picture strategy for how to. We have a deeply rooted and almost irreparably ruinous reputation to rewire.

That's the hope and key of the steps you're paging through and processing right now. It's an alarm and an atlas—a bullhorn and a handbook. I believe with all my heart it's God's cry and gift to His church to activate an approach that changes how we talk and who we talk to. People need to hear, know, and trust that's what they'll find when they come to God's house for healing.

---

62. See Exodus 20:5; 34:7; Deuteronomy 5:9; Numbers 14:18.

**We need to become the "Master Curators of Storytime,"** creating those spaces in our homes, at our dinner tables, and most urgently at the center of our churches, where anyone can know they can pour themselves out and tell any story, and they will be met with the unconditional and purifying love of God.

Please hear this: In a Real Talk environment, which is simply ushering back in all the biblical tenets, no one is going to say you're going to hell because of something you've survived or a choice you've made. That's where we get everything wrong. We're here to look at the pain that came before or that's living in you now. Some of the hills we choose to live or die on don't heal because we don't talk about the source or the solution. We just say, "Stop it," or "That was your past," but we don't provide the tools or the heart that lead to change. We're not breathing new life into one another, as we're called and gifted to do.

The tools in the conversation we're having here were created as a way to empower everyone—empower *you*—to find your position, step into your purpose, unpack who you are, learn how to use tools you didn't know you had, load up your arsenal of weaponry, and launch into an epic drama of purpose with intense God-armor on, shooting for next-level Marvel movie outcomes. Our kids aren't the only ones who need to hear that they're superheroes, under fire, but guaranteed to be more than conquerors when we run toward the battle like David—an ill-equipped laughingstock late bloomer, with spot-on spiritual aim.

When we let loose the armor God has put into our hands and step into the calling for which we think we're unfit (David's armor literally didn't fit), we not only change everything we see from where we stand, but we change the trajectory of the entire battle and everyone, every force involved with it, on both sides. Everything shifts.

David went from outcast runt to ready king. The surrounding soldiers shifted from fearful to free from their biggest foe. His entire nation tilted toward hope. In the time it took to sling a rock. Though the battle is lifelong and raging, *a shift can have a sonic boom of impact in a split-second of decision*—decision about whether or not you believe God can use you, that He wants to use you, if you would be willing.

Yes, it's scary. Yes, the enemy knows our weaknesses and is hell-bent (literal use) on stopping you. But God. God also knows, and He is the greater power and the final word. He knows the number of hairs on your head.[63] He knows more about your heart than you do. He knew everything already on the day He died to save you from all of this—and He did it anyway. There is no new information that will ruin the equation and make you unworthy of His power in the battle, because the battle is not based on you or your ability. It's based on the "same power" that raised Jesus from the grave and conquered death, which the Bible declares is available today—right now, in your circumstances—right where you stand.[64] His power can overcome any evil, even death. The only missing ingredient is your *yes*.

In or out, yay or nay, declining His offer and walking away as disappointed as the "very sad" rich man in the Bible[65]—or saying, "Bring it on!" According to the One who fights for you, you were born for this, and when you run toward the battle with His purpose in your hand, *everything shifts*.

---

63. See Luke 12:7.
64. See Ephesians 1:19–20.
65. See Luke 18:18–25.

# CHAPTER 8

# WHEN WE SHIFT, EVERYTHING SHIFTS

*It's not just about you; your change makes the same possible for others.*

There's a powerful illustration often used in talks and sermons about the impact of being off by one degree. The story compares results of such a miscalculation. On a 100-yard journey, you're only off target by about five feet, while that same miscalculation on a rocket's trajectory to the moon would leave you 4,169 miles off target, twice the moon's diameter. One degree.

There's another story about a flight from New Zealand to Antarctica in the '70s that had a two-degree error in flight coordinates, which placed them twenty-eight miles off course, completely unaware of a twelve-thousand-foot volcano in their flightpath. As a result of a minor shift in direction, 257 lives were lost. Two degrees.

I'd like to take a pause right here and really sink our teeth into this because there's urgency here in two different directions. There's the presumed positive interpretation of "everything shifting"—changing your life and others' lives for the better, which is the trajectory of this whole book, the Real Talk journey, and my life's mission. But what about what's lost if you don't course-correct? What happens when this is just a book you read and put down, if you don't choose to put anything into practice? What twelve-thousand-foot volcanoes are we hurtling toward unaware?

I'm passionate about helping people discover freedom and purpose. I'm just as passionate about seeing them separated from the cyclical pain of soul patterns and soul wounds.

> *WITH SUCH DISASTROUS CONSEQUENCES AT STAKE, IT'S AS URGENT AS TELLING SOMEONE TO DROP THE GUN.*

We need to do the work, set the stage of understanding that you have the ability to make a trajectory shift that moves results half a world away from where you're currently headed.

## SPIRITUAL GENOGRAMS

Genealogy and ancestry have become trendy in recent decades and often include the study of something called a genogram, which maps out your relatives' medical history, including hereditary patterns of behavior due to medical and psychological factors that run in the family. This isn't limited to diseases like diabetes or Huntington's. These are factors associated with alcoholism, drug addiction, anger management, mental illness, psychosis, and more.

Depending how you frame it, you could say my kids hit the jackpot of genogram dysfunction—nowhere to go but up, with awareness. Both sides are chock full of heartbreaking generational patterns, collectively: sexual addiction, infidelity, incest, several different manifestations of abuse (physical, emotional, verbal, sexual, spiritual), abortion, anxiety, cancer, domestic violence, homosexuality, and suicide. I list these in an attempt to go back and understand how to properly speak into my children's lives and sort out my own always-evolving layers in the process of redirecting the future. All of this, if left completely unaddressed and undealt with, is festering at best, and at worst doomed to be repeated.

In my family, as in many, the defense mechanism of the past is to simply "not see" these issues, not call them issues, or normalize them as typical (generational) family struggles. The only way to enter into true shift is when we realize the ability to see, admit what we see, and most restorative of all, admit what we see *to each other and declare,* "This stops here." That's a really hard step for most families to take. Real Talk attempts to do a deep dive into a spiritual-ties version of the genogram.

## ALL ALONE

I was so scared to tell my proud, stern, strongly opinionated Puerto Rican father that I had had an abortion. I was terrified. I played the preview reels of what I believed he would say and how I imagined he'd react. I thought I was about to change my relationship with him for the worse forever. But I was determined to work the steps, as they say, because it was changing me already, and I wanted more—to change myself more and to see change for my family, church, and world. So, I told him. And I could never have imagined what came next.

Like we see so many times in the Real Talk space—there were tears. Tears, and an apology, and heartache for what was lost because we (neither of us) had ever learned that "we need to talk." Profoundly and unexpectedly, he whispered, "That would have been my first grandchild," and with tears in his eyes, "Do you think we will ever see them?" This was beyond all I had hoped for, as it led us to talking about heaven and, *yes*, we have another beautiful child waiting for us there. He closed with a tenderness that surprised me when he said, "I'm sorry you were alone. I wish I could have been there for you."

There it was—the word of my childhood for far more than just my story about an abortion. *Alone.* I was alone in the aftermath of my sister's death. I was alone when I was abused, more than once. Alone in how I dealt with all of it: numbing, hiding, staying quiet, self-sabotaging— all while making sure everyone else was okay. I had no input or outlet. From the moment I lost my sister to the moment I lost my unborn child, I was alone, both in what happened to me and the decisions I made as a result.

One of the saddest parts was, upon hearing his reaction, I realized none of this had to be the way it was. If all of us had had the tools to talk, so much could have been different. If only we had a Real Talk pathway for a better understanding of these biblical principles.

I was moved by my father's emotion over this discovery. What gripped my heart the most was his comment, "This was my first grand-child." I realized in that moment it wasn't just about me. We were all missing out.

When my mother and I finally talked, like I mentioned in earlier chapters, she shifted in my mind from someone I never understood and who turned a blind eye to many of my childhood circumstances and environments, to someone who had lived through some of the same things and shut down emotionally in many of the same ways I had. It broke my heart to learn, only toward the end of her life, what she sur-vived, and that she, too, survived alone. I had had opportunities by now to unburden, confess, unpack my shame, know the truth of how I was known and loved, and find my purpose. Suddenly I went from feeling sorrow that my family hadn't given me this freedom sooner, to realizing no one had been there for them either. We were all alone, and we didn't have to be.

## BEAT IT OR REPEAT IT

From that discovery as a daughter, I pivoted toward the family I was given to build into as mother and wife, and I was relieved that I'd learned these things early enough, and intensely enough, that my kids' lives would be unrecognizably different. But why stop there? If God had His way, everyone I ever meet could have unrecognizably different lives.

It's generational backward and forward—healing from the ground zero of where you stand can spread healing to families, parents, influences from your childhood; it can heal your current adult relationships, marriages, community and work influences; it can heal your children and their future relationships and the paths they choose; and it can seal and cease the perpetuation of these bonds, lies, and habits, safeguarding new generations from continuing the cycle. It disseminates the smoke and mirrors not just from where you stand, but also allowing the world around you a clearer view of themselves and what God can do through their eternal purpose.

To get you there, we need to shift those patterns, cut those ties, rewire the roads we walk down. If you're ready to be honest and take a look at what's really going on behind some long-closed curtains, then you position yourself to become the change agent in an eternal story.

It only takes one. When one person, with one storyline, decides to shift, then everything your story is tied to, forward and back, begins to shift with you.

This means it only takes one to break a cycle. You could ignore all of this and continue old habits and generational patterns, or you could be the one. Beat it or repeat it. It's heartbreaking that it's that simple, and yet somehow the enemy knows how to keep us cycling, world without end.

If you and your purpose are not motivation enough, how about this: Your kids are watching. Beyond them, the world is watching—people you lead, people you love, people you aren't even aware of who notice the way you live, for better or worse. (Choose better.)

Well-known Christian speaker Corrie ten Boom tells a story of sharing the gospel with someone in a hotel room who didn't respond to her testimony at all, though she thought God had sent her to that place to share that message and that she was fulfilling a purpose. She was convinced, then disappointed, and that perceived failure stuck with her for a long time. Years later, when she was speaking half a world away to a crowd of thousands, she was approached eagerly after the event by a man who said he'd been searching for her across continents. He had hit his rock bottom once during an event in a hotel where he'd ended up passed out drunk in the room where Corrie was speaking of Jesus to others. Wrenched with guilt and covered in love, he wallowed in tears as he listened, gave his life to God then and there, went on to get sober and change his trajectory—and he had been looking for her ever since to tell her his story.

You never know who's watching—who's listening—but you do know that if you're operating within your purpose, if you're functioning in the center of God's will, then your purpose will find a way to be fulfilled and shift the world around you. Someone who matters is always watching.

I know what I took away from watching how my parents acted toward one another and their decisions, words, pain, and their unedited way of living this out in front of us. When they split, all the negative relational trauma was grooming me as a child to think, "This is okay." It was a large part of the reason I stayed silent in my issues as a child and why I "went along to get along" in my marriage regarding things I never should have gone along with. If you're not speaking up about what you're enduring, you're teaching kids and those around you that that's how they should react, and that's how they should be treated.

## *YOUR NEUROPATHWAYS BECOME REWIRED TO ACCEPT ABUSE AND NORMALIZE THE MESSAGE, "THIS IS OKAY."*

Now that I've traded my false coping mechanisms for God's true paths, what we normalize in Real Talk, I'm all the more aware that my kids are picking up on my and my husband's cues for what's okay and what the goal is in a loving relationship. If parents don't start to use the language of Real Talk with their kids, that means no one's speaking truth, no one's naming issues, and they're often overmedicating instead of doing the work of personal change.

If you do the research of the upswing of teens and young adults on medications in our current culture, you'll see it's skyrocketing disproportionately. It makes me wonder how much of that is just because of what's been left unspoken and how much of that can be redeemed and redirected through just a little authenticity in our parenting and relationships.

The cost is too great to take this flippantly and lightly—it's too great to be ignored and for us to continue in the same way. You're the key to deciding that this channel of damage is done. I'm thrilled that, for my family, I'm done, and I'm not passing any of the things in my past on to my children. The outcome is God's. We're not responsible for covering "the sins of the father,"[66] but we *are* responsible for opening and closing doors that affect change.

I should interject here to say, I don't blame my parents. I've processed a lot of how we got where we were:

---

66. See Exodus 20:5; 34:7; Deuteronomy 5:9; Numbers 14:18.

# *IT WASN'T INTENTIONAL—*
# *IT WAS GENERATIONAL.*

They didn't know how to communicate differently. No one gave them the tools, and they suffered many of the same traumas. But they had no idea how to break free and say, "I know this is happening to you. It happened to me too. I can relate." Or even better, speak to it in advance so it wouldn't be repeated. The bitterness, anger, and confusion we often hold onto about our upbringing isn't worth it. We have this opportunity and this gift to pause, cut off what holds us back, and give new generations a wide and healthy road to gain serious ground.

## FORGIVING SHIFTS THINGS

I can say with practiced confidence that in my lifetime, the cycle has been broken. And not just one. Once I saw the effects and realized the potential worldwide ripple effect, I went through the warehouse like gangbusters and lit it aflame, determined to break all the cycles—burn them to the ground and blow their ashes away.

I'm not afraid anymore of any of my stories or any new levels I might come against. There's not one part of me that spends one more second thinking, "Uh-oh, I hope *that* doesn't change how they think of me," or "If they only knew (what terrible things would happen)." It's all reconciled. The resulting transparency and reconciliation is part of why confession is so vital—and confession *to someone* (the Bible is very clear that when you confess "one to another,"[67] that's when your story has power). When your story becomes normalized, you carry a powerful tool to share!

---

67. James 5:16 KJV.

When Jesus healed people, they went and told somebody. Shift and shift. God gives us a healing, a gift, or a tool, and it changes us, but it's dead in the water if we do nothing with it. When we *use* it, when we "tell it forward," we move the world.

There's a serious need for all of us to get real and ask why we're afraid—and what we're afraid of. I can't stress enough: The greatest freedom over my past that I have is that I can walk into any room and, no matter who's in that room, be 100 percent comfortable with every aspect of my story. From a national podium to dinner at home with my kids. My kids are now adults, and I still mortify them with my honesty—but my prayer is that they avoid the suffocation of secrets or the isolation of going through a single valley alone. They're equipped, too, to lift others out of those valleys, even as young voices. In fact, they may be more powerful *because* they're young voices.

I use my story boldly as an encouragement not to let something name you and identify you. If you're struggling, it's because of the potential power in you and your ability to shift the world around you on its axis. You have greatness in you, and the enemy doesn't want it to come to fruition. He doesn't want you to get there. But you're holding a crystal-clear map in your hand that charts out a pretty short distance from point A to point "Be-loved."

## A NEW NORMAL

For eight chapters so far, you've been drinking from a firehose, and I know it's a lot. Some messages may seem like they are on repeat because, like the Bible repeats the important parts for emphasis, we've got to keep running the core messages through the loudspeaker until it's a new normal. "Do not fear," we are told 365 times in Scripture.

One of those repetition points is asking at every turn, "Are you ready?" This "ready," though, is different. The others were new and scary, filled with "first steps" and foreign concepts. By now you're growing into a pro, and the "ready" is a more powerful and prepared one. It's the "ready" of, "Put me in, Coach," and it's tied to a certain moment in the game where your skills (even if they're newly developed) start being able to move the ball down the field and affect the whole team around you.

Readiness is a common check-in that applies to each new level and Real Talk step. That's why in the "community of belonging," we've broken it down like graduating classes from 101 to 201 and on, and laid the discovery process out in the same five parts in this book. This is a ladder with very clear rungs, and thankfully, there are people now who have climbed it before you to lend you a hand.

Before we round the next bend (we're getting closer to the end), I encourage you to take a pause here—breathe—as you realize and bring into your heart that what you may have thought was all about you is actually so much larger than you. You're at the center of a thousand trajectories of eternal importance, and you're meant to do something with this. I don't want to put too much pressure on you about being one degree off, but I do want to encourage you toward what's possible if you hit your mark.

*As we shift into Part Four,* take a moment to prayerfully realize that what you're reading, processing, and preparing to walk out is already moving the climate around you. You want to check in personally with God here and get connected to His heart for where you're going and why. Your subtle change in spiritual temperature has the potential to pull a tornado-effect into motion, and it's about to touch down.

Be still—still as the eye of the storm—and know that He is God.[68] He is shifting these winds not to harm, but to move mountains. As you shift, *reflect* on how eternally and transformationally this is meant to influence your world—from those in your living room to those you don't even know who God is going to send your way. You are once again about to level up.

---

68. See Psalm 46:10: "Be still, and know that I am God."

# PART 4:

# RELEASE

# CHAPTER 9

# EMBRACING YOUR
# ETERNAL PURPOSE

*The very things you're afraid to talk about are going to be part of your purpose. The very thing used to try to stop you will be the thing God wants to use.*

When you finally understand that there's more, you can't settle for less. It's like the phrase, "Once you see it, you can't unsee it."

One of the questions Real Talk asks participants is whether they feel they're **living underneath their** purpose. Ninety-seven percent say yes (I say it's more like one hundred), with that 3 percent margin being people who doubt they *have* a purpose or that there could possibly be more. The 3 percent have little to no idea what they're capable of, unable to imagine the "unseen" things God could accomplish with, for, and through them if they're willing to step up and pay attention. Ultimately, yes, it's hard work, but starting isn't. Starting is just listening and being willing to ask the questions.

There's no question that you were made for more; we've more than established this. It's running on repeat throughout these pages and as this message reaches audiences around the world. When we get this far into the process, the new question is whether you're ready to pull the trigger and let everything be different. It's the point after the priest told me I should do penance, and I flinched at an unfamiliar and intimidating term. "Sure," I said while my *real* reaction was, "Surely, you jest." When he clarified by challenging me about why I wouldn't want to walk out and perfect my healing to truly heal, and in turn, help heal others— well, when you put it that way...

Still, stepping out can be the hardest part. I thought I would be embarrassed, kicking up more shame facing something so tied to my past (remember, he challenged me to help women not to make the same choice I'd made, which was way out of bounds as I had never spoken of my abortion). He pushed me way out of my comfort zone, but what would any of that have to do with finding my purpose? It was unrelated to who I am or thought I was. But that's what God was trying to show me. He had a different, broader picture of who I am than who I thought I was, and in His picture (always playing the long game), I was meant for a greater good. That was twenty years ago. Today, I can finally see the full purpose of that ask.

I had already done a lot of stepping out. I exposed some taboo truths, not just about my past but about my present, from my childhood to my marriage. If you are willing to look at it—into the gaping jaws of the monster, or into the mirror—and face it, whatever "it" is, it's not a long journey from there to complete deliverance and freedom.

It could happen in a click. Even if there have been a series of false starts, falling short, fearing a repeating cycle of "hope deferred,"[69] there's always a tipping point with an incredible invitation to jump. That's where everything changes. And it changes again at each new level.

---

69. Proverbs 13:12

You may have heard the phrase, "New levels, new devils," and it may be true, but what about, "New levels, new *revels*." In this journey to, through, and ultimately thriving within your eternal purpose, what if each new level of healing and helping brings you *new revelations you weren't even looking for* and could hardly imagine? What if we functioned, instead of with fear, from a place of intrigue and expectation for an unexpected deeper purpose?

A ministry that's yet to be born.

A relationship that's set to blossom.

A gift that's about to ignite.

A wrong you can right.

A flame you can light.

A purpose that explains your entire life.

What if you actually believed God when He promises that He has "plans to prosper you and...give you hope"[70] for a future chock full of reasons to be here? In that spirit, we're about to move from where we started (the awakening that you're "Made for More") to the permanent adoption of that truth as a way of life.

Why aren't we hungrier for this? If most of us (remember the 97 percent) have this "itchiness" for more, why aren't we more adamantly looking for what our unique personal purpose is?

*WE SETTLE FOR LIVING UNDER OUR PURPOSE BECAUSE IT'S EASIER AND DOESN'T HURT AS MUCH. OR SO WE THINK. BUT THE TRUTH IS, OVER TIME, IT'S FAR MORE PAINFUL.*

---

70. Jeremiah 29:11.

Fear of exposure is one of the enemy's most effective tactics. "It's awful out there. You don't want to be exposed. Stay inside. The world is waiting to take you down." We sit inside taking these arrows to the heart, mind, and body. If we'd just crack the door, his lie is all that would be exposed.

Instead of settling for less, let's let the idea of purpose and freedom settle in our hearts, settle on our spirits, and settle the argument, choosing how different and powerful life can be in God's hands for the rest of our days. This "settling" discovery is another level of letting go of that grenade you've been squeezing to death. That death grip is so much harder to maintain than releasing that cramped portion of your spirit and opening a hand instead to God's replacement—an explosion of goodness that you're ready and willing to trigger.

This is a process, and I encourage you to be prepared for it to take time. It did for me—but unlike me, you have the benefit of a Real Talk roadmap and a community. When I started in this season, there was no one to explain where I was going, how to get there, or the most effective steps to take. I was flying blind. Just one of the many reasons I'm so passionate about getting out in front of others, starting in kindergarten, and rolling out the red carpet, rich in purpose and refined healing.

In my personal story of progression, I was living a life that was immensely successful on paper, but I knew in my heart of hearts I was **not 100 percent in my sweet spot.** It was haunting me. Especially since I'd spent my whole life believing I was made for more. If I could have been blissfully unaware of a Creator's Divine Purpose, it might have been easier, but knowing it existed was killing me. I knew I was falling short and living underneath my purpose. If I was one degree off, it felt like total failure, and I was about 50 percent off.

When I had the encounter with the priest, I thought that was it. It was so comprehensive, and I felt so whole, what more could there be? Even when he explained the penance portion—the walking it out—that was just a formality, right? A pay-it-forward road toll that was about leaving the world better than you found it, right? I'd lived in Chicago and Florida—I know about tolls. They're just about access and egress. But *I* was good to go, yes? No.

Confession was just that first step onto the road we mentioned in chapter 7, "Born to Battle." Just like new levels and revels, there were worlds of healing to work through, and my purpose was hidden in that process, waiting to be untangled. There's a quote about discovery during penance by author Zora Neale Hurston that puts it perfectly, explaining, "There are years that ask questions and years that answer."[71]

For me, five years after that previous, powerful threshold of breakthrough, I was functioning but still operating in a deeply rooted habitual shame and not fully living as who I knew I was created to be. Some doors had instantly closed and never reopened, like pornography. That particular door was almost easy—instantly revealed, confessed, and closed. The occult as well—it terrified me as I now see it all differently and realize how it gets into our souls.

Others had varied shades of closure and understanding. I had walked out of that night of prayer, confession, and healing feeling exposed, but in a good way, knowing that I'd been healed, made whole. But so much didn't make sense, so much I didn't fully comprehend for decades. It was another uncorking of grief, so much unfelt, the start of years of feeling and grieving and releasing. "Years that ask questions."

In the next chapter, we'll cover the emotional exercise of unplugging trauma (which is sometimes an ongoing process), and we'll get deeper into "excavation." But we start the excavation process by *refining the healing*.

This is where you put a name to some of those strings that need to be cut—the traumas that need to be unplugged—and consider what they might have to do with your purpose. For me, this part of the process was like scraping out the inside of a pumpkin. I'd already dredged

---

71. Zora Neale Hurston, *Their Eyes Were Watching God* (New York: HarperCollins, 2000).

everything up and out for the purpose of confession, but what I didn't understand is that those things were unique tools. If I was going to live the life God gave me, I was going to have to look at them in a different light.

Now let's pause here because I'm probably confusing you, going back and forth from "don't pick it up again" to "definitely pick it up again," but note the fundamental difference: Don't pick up the shame and damage; do pick up the power of its purpose. Don't go back to the sin, which is remembered no more[72] and separated as far as the east is from the west.[73] Do realize you've been given a superpower unique to you. God doesn't waste a trial or challenge, so if it's something you've gone through, it's something He can redeem with a purpose—taking what was intended for your harm and using it for good.[74]

In the Bible, Joseph was tossed into an empty water tank (cistern) and left for dead until his brothers decided to sell him as slave labor instead—true crime better than *Dateline*.

## GOD DIDN'T JUST REDEEM THE SITUATION; HE USED THE SEPARATION.

This deep brotherly betrayal and life of abuse launched Joseph into his purpose as an overseer in the Egyptian government, positioned to deliver the people in his land from crippling famine and death. Including his brothers.

---

72. See Jeremiah 31:34.
73. See Psalm 103:12.
74. See Genesis 50:20 ESV: "As for you, you meant evil against me, but God meant it for good, to bring it about that many people should be kept alive, as they are today."

*WHATEVER YOUR CISTERN OF BETRAYAL
AND ENTRAPMENT, GOD HAS AN
OVERSEEING PLAN TO USE YOUR PAST TO
PROVIDE FOR YOUR FUTURE AND USE YOU
FOR A GREATER PURPOSE.*

When I got to a place of doing a complete internal inventory of what I'd brought up with the priest, what I'd let still fester over me for a few years emotionally even though God had cleared it out, I was finally ready for the work involved with the degree of life change that it would take to pursue my purpose.

It's all connected—what happened in your life, whatever needs to be purged. The very things you're afraid to talk about are going to be part of your purpose.

*THE VERY THING USED TO TRY TO STOP YOU
WILL BE THE THING GOD WANTS TO USE.*

For me, it had started with hiding my true pain, death, abuse, abortion, my heart hardening as the only protection I knew. The unearthing of the abortion led me to serve women in post-abortive trauma. Which led me to the realization that all of these women that I encountered had experienced some degree of sexual abuse and misuse in their lives. Which led me to create one of the fastest growing and highest impact anti-sex-trafficking organizations in the nation, which is still thriving today. As I talked to *those* women, I found the common ground of childhood abuse (note that early exposure to pornography is abuse), not believing they had worth and purpose, not realizing the darkness in their lifestyle was a symptom (dealing with a shame that wasn't even theirs), not having any place (including the church) to come for real, raw, open confession and healing—confessing what others had done to them. All of these things combined into the lightning bolt of Real Talk.

My own abuse, rape, promiscuity, abortion, numbing with alcohol, and porn in a devastating marriage—it all led to a program and process of healing and growing such a massive root system and churning the dead earth into fresh soil. What I needed to purge and burst into purpose—even better, it's the purpose of helping others to find theirs.

To guide you in this process a little, I shared an exercise in my book *Groomed* that you can easily do by yourself. It has proven incredibly revealing and useful for such a simple reflection:

Across the top of a blank sheet, label up to six columns, depending on your age now. Mark the first 0–7, the second 8–12, the third 13–17, the fourth 18–34, the fifth 35–49, and the last 50–present (stopping with the column that reflects your current age).

Under each column, list the most important events and memories you have from that age range. List both three to five highs and three to five lows, the memories that fill you with joy and the memories that still hurt to think about. Trust your discernment to bring the most important memories to your mind first, period. If you have a strong memory that doesn't feel like a high or a low, make a note of that too. These moments may not seem significant right away, but you remember them for a reason.

Perhaps the first thing you remember is going to your grandmother's funeral when you were four. Or maybe it's something that happened while you were playing with the neighbors in their tree house. Or it's the day your dad moved out of your house and in with his new girlfriend.

Give yourself time to recall details. What stands out? Is it something someone said? A motion you felt? Something you saw? Follow your memory as far as it goes. If you were playing in the tree house, what happened next? If your strongest memory from adolescence is the first time a boy kissed you, follow that event as far as you can remember. How did you feel in that moment? How did you feel later?

Don't second guess yourself, and don't ask anyone else what they remember. These are life events that are significant to you, and they'll be different from what your friends and family would list or remember. That's okay. Everyone registers and remembers events differently.

When you are done, spend some time with your list. These events groomed and shaped you for your future, which is why you still remember them. Winning a spelling bee in the 6th grade may have given you the message that you were smart and good with words, which affected your decisions to be on the school paper and eventually become a writer. The close friend who betrayed you in high school with your boyfriend, though, set you on a path of never vows that made you anxious and jealous in your relationships ever since.

When you put your past on to paper, you start to see it in a new way. Patterns emerge, and you start to ask, What are the pieces I love about my story? And, What are the pieces that still hurt to think about?[75]

---

75. Good, *Groomed*.

When you spend some time intently returning to these moments and tracing their thread into the thought processes and outcomes that surrounded them, you find the *why* behind your wiring, and some of the most pertinent influences behind your strengths and weaknesses. Follow that thread into your present, and you'll find where you need further healing, how you might relate to others in their hurt, how you can help, and how you respond in a way that could define your unique gift mix—secrets of the "you-niverse" you can put to use today.

It was this process of discovery that finally—seven long years later—moved me from self-transformation and spiritual deliverance to truly functioning within my God-given gifts. It helped me step up from a simple sense of believing I had purpose—if I could find it—to *living in and living out my eternal purpose.* "Years that answer."

To reach this point of breakthrough, it might take some struggle and challenge. But we already live in a set of struggles and challenges that do nothing but deteriorate us and the people around us. Instead of being stuck in painful memories, silenced shame, and destructive defense mechanisms (i.e., what worked before or coping skills you learned as a child), doing the work that unlocks eternal purpose defies and dissolves those false beliefs you've already been packing around for ages, and it unearths the aha moments you wouldn't have known to look for.

Whether you're naturally motivated by a search for purpose or not, it doesn't matter because there isn't a person on this earth who doesn't at least think about or wonder if "this is it"—if where they are is where they'll stay, and if what they were born for has already come and gone.

Major revelation: If you're still alive, then it has not.

The Bible says, "All the days ordained for me were written in your book before one of them came to be."[76] There's that eternal purpose again—stretching all the way back to before you were born. What an incredible promise and sense of being known. *You were intended.* That knowledge and intention stretches forward again to your "graduation"

76. Psalm 139:16.

from the earth, as God declares He has "determined" or "decided" the length of our lives on the earth.[77] If you are still here, you are still intentional.

Famed poet Oliver Wendell Holmes Sr. (who also happened to be a physician, which is especially poignant considering the healing effect of his words) once wrote, "A man should share the action and passion of his times at peril of being judged not to have lived." Gripped by the "peril" that it was to live but not really live, Holmes often wrote on this theme, and perhaps found a good editor, because he also said far more simply (and famously) that, *"Many people die with their music still in them."*

In the same (or greater) passion, the apostle Paul wrote to the Ephesians that, "We are God's handiwork, created in Christ Jesus to do good works, which God prepared in advance for us to do."[78] That's this chapter—and the core of Real Talk—in a single Scripture: We were created to "do good works." We have a creator-made purpose rooted in Christ. "Prepared in advance for us to do"—known, intended, called to "walk in" these words, as the verse is worded in the *English Standard Version*. Prepared and created on purpose for a purpose.

Even more beautiful, the root word behind the English "handiwork" from this verse, or "workmanship" as some translations say, is ποίημἄ (*poíēma*), which is etymologically related to *poème* or "poem." Following that thread, we—you—are God's poem.

*IF YOU DIE WITH THE MUSIC STILL IN YOU, THE WORLD IS ROBBED OF YOUR SONG, BUT MY HEARTFELT MISSION IS TO SEE TO IT THAT THE ENEMY CANNOT SILENCE THE*

---

77. See Job 14:5.
78. Ephesians 2:10.

## POETRY OF GOD THAT IS YOUR ETERNAL PURPOSE.

God created us to be able to feel that, and desire to live it out. That's the root of the unrest in most hearts that leads us to say, "I thought my life would be more meaningful. I thought having kids would make me happier. I thought I would eventually catch up to my peers and stop feeling so inadequate. I thought he or she would love me the way I long to be loved. I thought money, a job, that recognition...I thought...I thought..."

Everyone, if we're honest, has an "if only" or "I thought." It's one of the million ways we keep reassuring people, "You're not the only one." Take a moment here as we close up this chapter to be honest with yourself about your fill-in-the-blank—whatever it is that's selling you a "not enough" lie. Name it so you can face it and turn it into something divinely useful. Don't turn another page (literal or figurative) before you trade what burns in your heart for what can ignite your gifts. There is a glorious exchange rate when we bring our gifts to God in readiness:

## LAY DOWN YOUR LIMITED "I THOUGHT" AND REDEEM YOUR "I NEVER IMAGINED."

# CHAPTER 10

# NO GOING BACK

The middle is the hardest part.

When I got out of my marriage, I was in shock. I knew I couldn't go back, but I didn't know where I was going. I was humiliated. I thought I had put on a perfect persona. I had failed in my image, in my commitment, in my choices, and I hadn't been able to see this before it happened.

As people began to tell me how relieved they were for me, I realized I hadn't been fooling anybody, I had just been allowed to fool myself. It's a humbling process, but being able to adopt humility and adapt, I realized, was a bulletproofing step in healing.

When you're able to open your eyes and be honest about what is a fraud and a façade in your life, and get real, you let go of the fear that was holding you back. A tremendous weight lifts when you're not expending all that effort trying to keep a lid on your problems. Blow the lid off. Stay humble (impossible to do this any other way). Live free. And do not, under any circumstances, turn back.

As you're going through this awakening process, you discover at each level that there's no going backward. This is a lot of work, and it takes time. You don't want to have to do it twice.

"No going back" is the next step in your healing process. This is where it's impossible to go it alone—you need your army, your support system. We said before that *confession* is a scary word, but *accountability* can be even scarier.

With *confession* at least you're speaking of things that are behind you, mistakes in your past. Even if your past was last week, at least you're sending the message that you know you messed up and you're moving on.

*Accountability* is more like turning on the florescent lights over your personal life, inviting someone to get all up in your business and call you to the mat on your messes. Who wants to live in that kind of spotlight? It's nice to have a few dark little corners to hide in when you need to go off duty and let your guard down. An escape hatch. Breathing room. I'm going to walk it out for sure, but don't watch me so closely. Accountability is a raw light to live in.

As hardcore as accountability is, it doesn't have to be complicated: Ask people to tell you if they see anything out of order. Speak out as soon as you know you have done something that falls into old patterns—or better yet, when you are even thinking about it! When you feel that old thought, desire, motive creeping back in, tell on yourself. It saves so much time! Create your own board of personal advisors. Essential: Put God at the head of it.

This is not a man-led task force where you shift from the enemy's voice to man's as the voice of authority in your life. It's important that this is a Spirit-led partnership. You should only attempt accountability with those you determine are sincerely, authentically aligned with the Holy Spirit. Any time you are following another's lead in a Christian leadership or relationship situation, it works best when you are submitted to someone who is fully submitted to God. That means they're leading and influencing from a place of humility and in lockstep with divine direction. We all ebb and flow in our spiritual health, but knowing someone strives for that kind of relationship with God is something you want to put in check as a starting place. Like the saying, "Only follow a pastor who's following the Master."

So again:

Create your own board of personal advisors.

Put God at the head of it.

Ask Him to excavate and show you what you need to see or do.

**Excavation** is the key to this almost-home-free step. The enemy wants to keep us from tripping the wire that sends us to the next level. God wants to set us right in front of it and get us up and over the top in this incredible, "unspeakably good" journey.

As you move through different breakthroughs and discoveries and stay the course, it's essential to excavate and make sure there are no leftovers. This is where we really implement the concept introduced in chapter 2 ("Made for More") about "bringing the last 2 percent to the table."

By means of refresher, the "last 2 percent" is the leadership theory that people leave things unsaid during meetings, experiences, and conversations, for whatever reasons, including fear of rejection or looking stupid. Self-doubt and the insecurity of having nothing to offer or the feeling of being invisible cause us to remain silent. Good leaders are able to draw this 2 percent out of a person, knowing that's usually their most important "first 2 percent" they walked in thinking and wanting to share. That essential tier is traditionally where you find someone's *"made for more" core.*

The reason we're revisiting it is exactly because of the "first/last 2 percent" principle—the thing you walked in with *is* the thing left on the table at the end. Excavating the last 2 percent nails down the victorious work you've put in so far.

I speak from experience—I had to *do* the work and pave the way. I was challenged to do so and expected to live it out. If you remember from chapter 5, "The Lost Art of Confession," I didn't initially think I would. I had a once-in-a-lifetime encounter with the priest, but then I was given an environment for the next seven years where the Lord gave me a way to walk it out.

I was grieving. I transitioned to Florida with the hope of "doing nothing" for a while after such an expense of my soul had been poured into ministry and clinical work for so many years before. But God was steering me toward a work that would heal my war wounds in a far better way than being still.

Learning to walk it out is hard. It's easy to go back to what you know. It's hard *not* to go back to the familiar. We see it in human nature and in Scripture. There's a reason for the phrase "like a dog returns to its vomit."[79] There's a tragic sensation, watching the Israelites in the Bible want to revert to the slavery from which they were freed, all for the craving for an onion. Violence, death, oppression, 430 years enslaved, and so many miracles unleashed to set them free—the visible hand of God in their deliverance, as death passed over their households, and His Spirit indwelled a pillar of cloud for them to follow, filled with fire by night. Barely two months in, they had forgotten the "experience" and given up on walking it out. The grumbling threw away the gift. Like Esau gave up his blessing for soup,[80] they decided their mountains of miracles were "meh" in comparison to "pots of meat" and our fill of bread.[81]

Even more embarrassing and convicting in its relatability, God met them in their weakness with yet another miraculous provision. Manna from heaven, falling like dew. Full provision of all their daily needs. So now, they've seen enough to ensure "no going back," yes? Sadly, no. They

---

79. See Proverbs 26:11–12.
80. See Genesis 25:29–34.
81. See Exodus 16:3–4.

looked their latest miracle in the eye and said, "There's nothing to see but this manna!" More interested in a Food Network of lesser opportunities, they "wept," the Word says, over strong cravings unfulfilled.[82] Temporal things that were their comfort foods. "Who will feed us meat? We remember the fish we ate freely in Egypt, along with the cucumbers, melons, leeks, onions, and garlic. But now our appetite is gone; there is nothing to see but this manna!"[83] God has given us nothing—except everything we need. We are, all of us, that ungrateful.

What manna has fallen in your life fresh from His hand? Though you may be in your wilderness and unsure about your future, you know He's showing up for you with more than enough to get you where you're going. You're headed away from the land of your captivity and toward a permanent freedom, but you have to keep moving in the right direction. He knows what draws us, though, and spoke to that felt need, promising a "land flowing with milk and honey."[84] We think we're missing onions when He's trying to lead us to honey, and all we have to do is follow Him and not turn back. It shouldn't be this hard.

But it is, for a few reasons. Remember what we learned in chapter 7, "Born to Battle"? Satan won't drop his purpose until he's stolen ours. He whispers leeks and onions to us when we're eating Wheaties in the desert. He lies to us about the soft landing of going back to our vomit and taking the easy road. But it's not an easy road at all—it's a cycle of soul patterns that keeps us spiraling and circling the drain.

Remember what we said about him hitting you in the same open wound, so it won't heal? If there's something you are convicted about doing differently, and you go back to it, that wound opens even wider. Part of the reason it's so hard to stay in your journey with open vulnerability, able to garner help and support along the way, is that people are so judgmental. People in general, the people in your life, you—you can be the most judgmental toward yourself. Unfortunately, many Christians

82. See Numbers 11:4.
83. Numbers 11:4–6 BSB.
84. Deuteronomy 31:20.

are the most judgmental of all when, if we really understood Christ's love, we'd be the least. Let's own this weakness. We can't fix it unless we do. That's what Real Talk is for on both sides.

So let's get real about this for a second.

The world says, "Christians are so hypocritical." And they're right. You have someone whose coping mechanism is food eating their way through their problems while shaming someone for living with her boyfriend. We act like we're tacked down while pointing fingers at more "visible" sins, things that are more definable, public, exposed. Things we've risen up against with a mob mentality. But people did the same thing to Jesus, saying, "Crucify that guy! He's got it wrong. Give us the murderer Barabbas instead." We've been pointing our fingers since time began, stealing others' ability to heal, hiding from our own need to heal, and putting anything Christlike in a tomb while the enemy's murderous plot roams free in our lives. Will we never learn? Will we never get real?

There's a poem called "Autobiography in Five Short Chapters" by Portia Nelson, used in the Alcoholics Anonymous *The Big Book*, that maps out the stages of change and "undoing auto pilot," as we've said, in utterly convicting simplicity. In **step one**, someone walks down the street, falls into a deep hole, and sinks into hopelessness and despairs of ever getting out. "It's not my fault," they say. In **step two,** they walk down the same street and "pretend" they don't see the hole. Same outcome, deeper shame because, how can we let the same thing happen again? Still, they deny any fault. **Step three** has us walking down the same street, same hole, same fall, but this time, there is ownership and an opening of the eyes, admitting this is a habit and it's entirely my fault. Knowing the environment, though, they get out immediately. **Step four,** same street, new behavior, they walk around the hole. **Step five,** they choose a new street. That's when there's finally no going back.

It's a great analogy, but in real life (and Real Talk), how do we suddenly change behavior and avoid the street and climbing down into that old familiar trap in which we've spent so much of our life?

## UNPLUGGING TRAUMA

One of the many tools you'll find in Real Talk is a walkthrough of *unplugging a trauma*. I also shared this in my book *Groomed*, where one of our trauma doctors, who played a pivotal role in my personal journey, taught me that "nobody would care about past experiences if those weren't somehow negatively affecting you now." He goes on to explain that we still feel guilt, shame, and trauma from past experiences because when we think of them, the way our emotions and synapses work, we return to the emotional development of that moment and our brains think it's happening to us again in the present. Our mind has no way of differentiating chemically a memory versus an experience. We're not going to be able to feel differently about that subject or life history until the memory is "acknowledged and unplugged," he shares. "Then the emotional charge is gone and [you're] not haunted by it anymore." You accomplish this by staying intentionally emotionally present while remembering the past, and consciously "uncoupling" from the emotional memory, realizing it's not current, live, or repeating at any time, now or in the future. You unbox the realization that you don't have to have that emotional memory.

It sounds too simple, but that's what the experience with the priest did for me. When you work with the right partners and bring in the power of the one true Holy Spirit, it is shocking how quickly things can shift. As mentioned in the last chapter, I had been carrying around a constant emotional grenade of shame, fear, regret, anxiousness, and keeping my hand so tight around the release lever just trying to keep everything from exploding. It was exhausting, and I didn't even realize I was doing it.

When someone points this out to you, helps you open your hand and release the grenade you've been strangling for a lifetime, there's this rewiring moment of confusion and observation as you notice that it never engaged. No carnage. It's a dud. You could have let go long ago! Now it's dead on the table, harmless—if you let it be. Just don't pick it up again.

Be advised you're going to be tempted to pick up again everything you put down. We've touched on this before. It's one of those messages on repeat that applies to every level you're going to walk through, and it's one of the benefits to getting a Real Talk-style support system around you. You're going to need partners and coaches around you to shout plays from the sidelines and a team of cheerleaders to help you up your game.

You're going to be pulled on, and things are going to break. It's going to make you want to stop, give up, turn around, go back. When there's "no meat," when a thousand Egyptian chariots are raining down, you'll think about going back, and maybe you'll want to. What people need to know is that when you first start walking through the Real Talk steps, it's like walking through sludge (and for some, being hit by a sledgehammer—I know; inviting). It's weird, hard—and you might hate everything about it. But that's because you don't have the muscle memory for this new way of walking. It's all new. You're wonky and wobbly like a newborn baby. Maybe a newborn calf. That's why you need to build an army around you. If you don't have that type of support system in place, we help you build it in Real Talk, and in part, show up as participants ourselves in your Real Talk team.

We accomplish this with a full-time online community keeping us all connected. I still need that connection too. In the Real Talk journey, I'm in that community with you, walking this out live every week with all our partners around globe, who all have different gifts in them, and who carried me and equipped me to stay in my healing and get where I am.

When I first created these groups, I wasn't sure if they were making a difference until I started hearing people share after they participated. The impact on those people, and the inspiration of their commitment, is part of why I pivoted immediately and haven't gone back. It hasn't been all roses. But most relationships, the ones the Lord has kept in my life, have been transformed. I think it's fair to say, part of it working depends on the rapid exit of some people from your life, those who don't fit where you are going. As we've read, the rippling Real Talk effects and literally "real talk" that I've been able to take home to my family, all generations, has unleashed a healing backward and helping forward.

It's human nature to want things to be easy and to default to the simplest conditions. It's also understandable when we give up, because change hurts. But transformation never happens in the comfort zone. The enemy makes it hard and tempts you to quit because the minute you cross this threshold and become the change agent, willing to say, "This is worth it," you are making a push for breakthrough.

The key is letting the Holy Spirit have free reign. He has the keys to all the doors. God offers the key to freedom, and we turn it down! We say no thanks because of vain imaginings. We project the future based on our past, our fears, our negatives; but what if we projected a future about Jesus, with the hopeful expectation that we know He's going to equip us to walk through whatever we need to live free in Him? Saying yes to the wilderness is often the only way through to a promised life of freedom.

When something in you finally says this is not okay—and that everything is going to *be* okay if you take the difficult steps—something cracks open, everything in you changes, and when it does, there's no putting that genie back in the bottle; there's no going back. It's a method of living you can apply at all times and to all pieces of your life moving forward, each time you're leveling up.

The tool that gets you to this point of no return and gives you an uplift, to move you through a constant upcycling, is an advanced version of learning to "speak the unspeakable." When you make this your new normal, a new soul pattern, a new way of living, that's when you cross a border and step into the Good Life.

# PART 5:

# RELAUNCH

# CHAPTER 11

# THE GOOD LIFE

Welcome to the Good Life. Yes, you do deserve it.

When I married Mr. Good, a lot changed. I don't credit my husband as the *sole* reason for the life change—I give full credit to God for aligning all that I was going through at that time. This scriptural process was yet to be laid out in an easy-to-access, step-by-step biblical process, which we now call Real Talk.

I've learned to give myself due credit too for the hard work of pursuing change, refusing to settle for less, and not going back. It's hard to give yourself credit and celebrate your wins! But you know what? It is essential. Pause and take it in. Celebrate you!

But back to Mr. Good. The one piece I hadn't learned yet at that time was how different life and marriage can look with a "Good" partner. The slow-burn part was how surprisingly hard it was to truly release former trauma and trust stepping into the Good that God had provided. It would take me a while to make all the connections in the analogies that God was writing in inviting me to take on a new, Good name.

I'll let you in on a little secret (wouldn't be the first time): I even struggled for months over what version of my name or names to go with for the cover of this book. It was a simple question—what name did I want to choose? How did I want my name to "appear" (so much sub-text in that wording)? Elizabeth. Melendez. Fisher. Good. It opened a Pandora's box of self-(re)discovery.

It wasn't for any simple or superficial reasons. There were some deep identity questions happening:

**Melendez** carries my heritage and is tied to my culture and the style of my upbringing that is such a crucial part of everything I've been sharing with you in this book.

**Fisher** carried in it pieces of my heart for my kids, keeping my name identical to the surname they'd been born with. Until they graduated, I wanted to be their mom noticeably, like rooting for Max Fisher in football, or replying to simply Mrs. Fisher, as their mom. I told my youngest I wouldn't change my name until he was out of high school, as it's nice to have your mom match you. I lived that with my own mom, and it meant a great deal. Honoring my children with recognition and likeness has been very important to me.

**Good**. Was I? Was life finally Good? Was I Mrs. Good? Was I deserving enough? Was I ready for that name covenant? Like honoring my kids, I also wanted to honor all that my husband was to me and had brought into my world, declaring "I'm all in," right down to our shared name.

Under all of these, there was this fast-moving current of coming to grips with truly letting go of my past and realizing (almost disappointingly after thinking I'd grown more than that by now) how much I did not believe I deserved the Good life—literally or figuratively.

Literally, I didn't believe I deserved this good, good man who loved me so differently than anything I'd ever known. Still functioning from a place of having been groomed in all sorts of problematic ways as a child—groomed for appearances, to be invisible, to endure (i.e., settle for any kind of treatment and not realize the fine line between strength and abuse), for judgment, and with financial fear—I considered all those categories a checklist of worthiness, and I was falling short (IMHO) of each and every one. I wasn't patient enough, accomplished enough, healed enough, softened enough. What did I have to offer that would be the proper "payment" for love and belonging? But I had met someone who so exemplified the straightforward unconditional love of Christ in our relationship that I found myself eliminating the checklist one by one. I still struggle now and then as old habits die hard, but it is not for lack of evidence that I was finally fully accepted and fully loved, just as I am.

Figuratively, the symbolism was really throwing me for a loop, making me prayerfully face a few leftover dark corners where I was hiding from the upheaval of healing that God was still waiting for me to embrace. I've been in my healing how many years now? And there are still stories God puts before me as a devotional of life discovery.

It took me a long time after I got married to legally change my name to Elizabeth Good. I finally did, but I didn't realize till working on this book how much the proverbial change was in lockstep with the legal change. It had taken me a very long time to embrace my new, good, *spiritual* name, identity, and covering.

The reason that journey becomes a part of this book is because not recognizing our worth is so typical for all of us. It can be one of the most insurmountable parts of the process for anyone I work with:

**Phase One:** I see people willing to run to the end of the diving board and spring into the deep end, even from the high dive, the minute they hear someone relate to their sin, struggle, or saving grace. "Me too!" "I thought I was the only one!" "I've never told anyone this before." The confessions and tears and bold exchanges come hard and fast, one after another. People are *ready* for Real Talk. Starved. They take it in their arms, running like the woman at the well[85] to tell others so they

85. See John 4.

can hear it too and be set free. "No one's talking like this." "The church needs this." "This is the key to changing everything." These reactions don't take time; they're immediate and urgent.

**Phase Two:** The part that takes time was being symbolized by my Good name change: It was hard to believe it was for me. It's hard for people to believe the new seasons and true outcomes are for them. It was easy to take the first step, but hard to excavate the deepest pools of doubt and defeat.

## HABITS ARE HARD TO LEAVE. WORTHINESS IS HARD TO BELIEVE.

But right here is the final turning point of living in your eternal purpose. Not just understanding you have purpose, or discovering the first steps of what that purpose is, but thoroughly immersing yourself in your purpose as a totally changed way of life.

This is still an important Real Talk step to walk through and an essential conversation to have because it's not as easy as just "knowing" these things and moving into your new "good life" digs. There are still more excavations and explorations to be done in a few key areas to really get this understanding into your muscle memory. (Keep going—we're almost there.)

## A GOOD LIKENESS

Here I was developing this systematic pathway and believing in it wholeheartedly, so it was a surprise to discover there were pieces of me that thought my own healing was counterfeit. It was subconscious more than conscious. There were places that I still struggled with, and I still doubted myself.

Believing in the good life, resting in it, and enjoying living in it is where you are no longer waiting for the other shoe to drop. You finally adopt a new line of thinking where vain imaginations are far less—the enemy's never going to stop trying to convince us of the lie that the worst is coming. This is a never-ending work of faith to keep walking the walk and talking the (real) talk.

Embracing the counterfeit is why I stayed in my old ways so long—in my old marriage and relationships. I always believed things would shift for the better, believing in people and outcomes even when others didn't. The fine line between being hopeful and being deceived is a big growth hurdle.

It's very hard *not* to settle for a counterfeit or false hope and to wait for good, better, best until our radar is honed, our messaging tweaked, and our eyes fully opened. Be encouraged, this is one of the most common issues for any human being in any area of our lives. It's the number one reason that people get into or stay in bad relationships, toxic jobs, not stepping out into something they think God is calling them to do. It's so easy just to go with "good enough" or "leave well enough alone."

Counterfeits work in both directions when we also struggle with thinking we, ourselves, are counterfeits. "What a phony, fake, failure. If anyone could see all of me!" It's a very common disease, as we can see by the meteoric rise of the trending term "Imposter Syndrome" in recent years.

It is hard to shake yourself from the traditionally negative side of self-doubt—but I'm also going to suggest something to you that you're going to want to underline and might find just a little offensive. There's a big part of us human beings that is comfortable in our messes. Whether it's due to familiarity or fear of change, we get way too comfortable in whatever habits or role we've taken on, in the bed we've made, lured and lulled into a false sense of security and covering. It's one thing to be skittish about getting out of the boat and walking on water[86]—an

---

86. See Matthew 14:22–33.

"unbelievable" feat. It's another thing to be snuggling deeper into the bow of the boat with our back to the waterfall, careening to an edge we know will end us.

## GOOD GRIEF

Not only are counterfeit ways, and counterfeit self-images, hard to change and walk away from, but there are several good (understandable) reasons for this—one of which is having to go through a surprising process of grief.

You'll often hear people who have gone through a traumatic season of relational loss, betrayal, or divorce say that it feels like a death—yet we don't pause and give ourselves the time to truly grieve or feel it all. Turning in a new direction and letting go of the old requires a mourning process, even when you know it is ultimately for your own good.

Further, when you step into a new season, filled with positive change, it comes with an often-unexpected groundswell of grief when you realize how you were living before, how much it stole from you, how you wish you'd realized all of this much sooner, and how much ground you have to cover to get to a truly excavated, healthy place. When the light comes on and we see the carnage all around us—oh, the devastation! We mourn when we face the truth that we weren't living at that level the whole time, realizing we were living beneath our purpose all along, and time was lost. There's grief in that.

But there's a beautiful completion to stepping into something new, even when your heart is breaking a little and letting go. You'll know you're ready if you can say there are parts of life you definitively regret or feel grief over when you think about how it played out—that's when you're actually able to pivot because you can see the previous conditions for what they were.

That's different from being so steeped in an unhealthy way of living that you can't see its brokenness. "It's fine. I'm okay." "I've got this." "He doesn't mean it." "She will change." When you come out the other side, your words will change to: "I can't believe I didn't see it." "How did I endure for so long?" "Why did I allow that?" "Why didn't I see it?" Literally, "I feel like I can breathe!"

It's not about making you feel regret or being against the idea of living with "no regrets," trusting Romans 8:28 where God promises He works all things together for *good*. It's just about calling brokenness what it is and not making excuses for Satan's weak but destructive disguises. We have to name it and leave it.

## THERE'S GRIEF IN CHANGING FROM CALLING EVERYTHING PERFECT TO ADMITTING IT'S NOT.

*It's a good grief, though.* I encourage you to go ahead and dwell in it—let the grief be a positive sign of forward movement. It's an indicator that you're different now. "I can see clearly now the rain is gone." Even if you're still in it, barely out of it, or holding on, start to make friends with the idea of grief. It's a badge of honor that says you're headed for good things. It's a bevy of spotlights showing you where the good way is and at the same time allowing you to celebrate that, yes, you can see it. If you can see the lights cutting through the dark, then you can see the dark for what it is.

Even if there's one area, relationship, choice, secret, or situation, one unspeakable thing you've never come clean with, one story that still, deep down, defines you internally in a way that just doesn't feel good—you can be sure that there is purpose and that God can and will use every bit of it now for this next level. And it's going to be so worth it.

## LOOKING GOOD

Most of the time I'm pretty encouraging and supportive in the way I talk through these concepts—blunt, yes, because you have to be when you're dealing with what we're dealing with. Real talk is blunt by definition. But generally we cheerlead people through the process. There are also a few things that merit a good, swift kick in the pants, and this is one of them: For this to work, you're going to have to get over yourself a little.

So many years, I passed up the offramps of truth and freedom that God offered me because there was no way I was going to drop the façade and admit defeat and imperfection. If it dug my grave, I couldn't let on. We all make compromises and settle, in countless ways. On the night with the priest, worry about my image could have stolen my purpose one last time if I'd let it get in the way. Remember, my beautiful, "perfect" friends were standing witness to my seeming demise while I lit my life on fire in a rolling wheelbarrow. But light it I did, and once I started, I kept throwing logs onto the pile. I had to get over myself; this mattered more.

It is an ongoing life process, so don't be discouraged. We spent a whole chapter on this in "Born to Battle," making it clear that:

*SATAN WON'T DROP HIS PURPOSE UNTIL HE'S STOLEN OURS.*

As long as you're here, you're a target simply *because* God has a plan for you. Another backward badge of honor. And you're going to need help with that like we all do.

This is where we need support and community. One of my rocks is a very special woman named Lynne Jubilee (yes, she changed her name too). I like to call her "my rabbi." She's a patient, humble, valiant warrior who pours into leaders on the world stage. She started as a prayer counselor in a Billy Graham prayer tent at thirteen, and she says she felt assigned to me by God. Assigned. Well, you know what? I took her up on it! There were days I would tell her how I would wake up filled with dread, paralyzed by questions of, "Who's going to be against me today? What am I going to face that I can't handle?" I leaned into her, believing that she actually *was* sent to me to be that support.

> THERE ARE PEOPLE ASSIGNED TO YOU. IF YOU'RE WILLING, THE LORD WILL ALIGN YOU TO THEM.

I look back on my life and can't believe the synchronicity of who God has put me in front of, when, and why. The same goes for every relationship and circumstance that came together to get this book in your hands. If you have nothing else to go on, let that be one not-so-small piece of evidence that God's already assigning people to *you*. We're here. We're working on this together. Then there's the Real Talk community we mentioned in the last chapter; if you don't know where to start with putting together your own board of directors or advisors, as we've mentioned, just start with the community we've already gathered and prepared for you.

Of all the things that easily deter us from leaning into that help, don't let image be one of them. Whatever your sticking point, embrace it. I had a tough time with my Spanish heritage growing up in the northwest suburbs of Chicago. The crass things I heard my grandmother being called on our own front lawn, the shocking racism of peers in high school. I watched as my dad tried to hide from this, going out to restaurants and giving his last name as "Mel." I found it a great haven to move to the Miami-Fort Lauderdale area late in my teens and blend into a sea of Melendezes, Garcias, and Hernandezes!

People embrace labels so easily—they look for any way to make you feel bad and join in the story or accusation about who you are (and we tend to readily do this to ourselves as well). It also makes us struggle with our own worth and ability to be chosen by God to do anything. We feel broken or question why God wouldn't change things on our behalf. This concept plays out time and again in the Bible and is gaining steam culturally because of the *Chosen* franchise playing a scene out beautifully between Jesus and "Little James." The scene on disability went viral because "it resonated with so many people."[87]

Little James approached Jesus, humbly challenging, "You're sending us out with the ability to heal the sick and lame, so you're telling me that I have the ability to heal? I just find that difficult to imagine, with my condition, which you haven't healed."

Jesus: "Do you want to be healed?"

James: "Yes, of course, if that's possible."

Jesus: "I think you've seen enough to know that that's possible."

James: "Why haven't You?"

Jesus: "Because I trust you."

Jesus goes on to explain that physical healing is a great story, but it's been told. James, He says, will have a greater story in discovering the genuine ability to praise God in spite of his disability. When James understands this, his challenge changes from "Why not my healing?" to "Why would You love me that much?" He wonders why God would trust him to serve in this way when others are better, more "fearfully and wonderfully made."[88] But Jesus replies:

You are going to do more for Me than most people ever dreamed. So many people need healing in order to believe in Me. That

---

87. *The Chosen*, season 3, episode 2, "Unlawful," directed by Dallas Jenkins, written by Ryan Swanson, Dallas Jenkins, and Tyler Thompson, aired July 4, 2021, https://new.thechosen.tv/.

88, Psalm 139:14.

doesn't apply to you.... When you find true strength because of your weakness, and when you do great things in spite of this, the impact will last for generations.

How many of us are walking "slowly and with a limp"? How many are asking, "What do you mean I'm called to greatness, when I'm not even getting by?" I went through a 180 similar to the one in the James story during my experience with the priest, going from not even knowing how truly broken and in need of healing I was, to receiving the humbling surprise of being chosen for transformation.

There's incredible beauty in just showing up and doing this work in an authentically imperfect human way. How much greater is the testimony of God's power when we just show up in our weakness, with our limp, with the world, the enemy doing what he does best as the accuser of the brothers, and say, "I am ready for more"? We don't even have to know what the *more* is, but we can admit we are done with the pain, the hiding, and the cacophony of lies, fears, weakness, and insecurity.

There's so much in a name, but you have to be vigilant and watch which name you're working under and what it says to you. Is it a name (label) you gave yourself that you need to shed? A name given to you by your enemies that you need to reject? The names you give to your demons, normalizing what is not meant to be normalized? The name you give to your problems, making them bigger than you? You are not your past; you are chosen, and you have many gifts and promises still to unpack.

The good name *God* gives you—that's the one you want to put in lights that shine so bright they drown out all the rest. Blinded by the light.

## USED FOR GOOD

Moving past the work of unworthiness, the next question you need to ask yourself is a harder, more honest one: If it means walking in your limp, are you willing to walk that out to get to the good life?

When I was starting to do the first Real Talk pilot groups, there were tons of people going through it and responding incredibly, yet the lie in my head was that people weren't getting anything out of it. It went against all the evidence staring me in the face, but I still believed it. I knew that I needed to hold my head high and keep doing what the Lord told me to do, and I kept telling myself, "The enemy is a liar and the only one behind the words that tell you you're not *good* enough." That's when I learned this perspective war is *part of the equation* that brings the punch. Understanding that when we are weak, He is strong.[89] *He* placed that dream in you. It may still be unspoken, but it is intentional, and it's time to jump into discovery and fuel up for adventure.

I want you guys to get this:

> *YOU HAVE TO WALK INTO THE ROOM THAT YOU DON'T WANT TO WALK INTO BECAUSE IT'S TYPICALLY A LIE THAT'S KEEPING YOU OUT OF IT.*

The best way to discover that truth and disarm the devil is to go busting into the proverbial room of whatever you're facing. My whole life I've fought the voices and circumstances that have knocked me off my feet. I suffered the most horrific losses but had the most beautiful breakthroughs. I would hear, "You don't matter, everybody hates you," and simultaneously get to walk in unprecedented favor. You have to believe that God has prepared a table for you in the presence of your enemies.[90] And He always will! You just have to take the room.

---

89. See 2 Corinthians 12:10: "That is why, for Christ's sake, I delight in weaknesses, in insults, in hardships, in persecutions, in difficulties. For when I am weak, then I am strong."
90. See Psalm 23:5: "You prepare a table before me in the presence of my enemies. You anoint my head with oil; my cup overflows."

The same battle of the voices will still get me now in my fifties. Something wonderful will happen, and something will try to steal it. People will turn on you and betray you, but the Judases that catapult you to your next situation are providentially positioned. The enemy will always use a person who doesn't have the wisdom and discernment to see the truth. When he does, God also sends a person—and an army behind them. Listen to the army and believe their encouragement.

When someone's walking with God, they don't lead with accusation, they lead with reconciliation. Besides, the slings and arrows we get from people aren't about us anyway. They're about the brokenness in them, people who don't know their identity and want the favor that's attached to us. What people don't know is that they can't take your favor. It's yours. It's just yours.

## THE GOOD WAY

Why did it take so long for me to understand this "good" identity and figure out why I was resisting it when it was being handed to me on a silver platter? The first few years of my new marriage, I always told my husband, "You are helping to heal my brain." New neural pathways needed to form in my and my children's brains after the lifestyle we'd endured. All of us were settling into the good life slowly but surely, and it took work. Allow time for the chaos to clear.

Now I head into every year with tremendous growth. I started a foundation, I met my husband, I created a tool that has potential for major change. I'm walking in my purpose. So now, when you look at the cover of this book and you see my name, it says simply, "Elizabeth Good," because you know what? This is who I am. The Lord has given me yet another new season and "next level," and it's good. I'm excited to finally walk this out in a good way. To live, love, and believe that I deserve this "good" gift.[91] No more vain imagination, looking over my shoulder, waiting for the other

---

91. See James 1:17: "Every good and perfect gift is from above, coming down from the Father of the heavenly lights, who does not change like shifting shadows."

shoe to drop. I am simply settling into the good life. As I've been doing since the introduction of this book, I'm going to keep inviting you to do the same, because if this isn't about me, and it's all from God, that means it's for you in the same way and to the same measure.

At this writing, I'm over half a century old. It took this much of my life, but now the clouds have cleared, and the fog is lifting more and more every day. I know my calling clearer than anything in the world. I understand every battle along the way, which is why I'm vehemently passionate about helping people understand their own battles and the supernatural ability to whittle them into weapons to be used for good. Everything that happens or has happened to you that wasn't good was intentionally designed and sent to take you off course. If you take the time to pay attention and look at what happened, the patterns created and how they've been playing out, you'll start to see this tactic clearly—and you can't see the tactic without seeing your worth. If you're worth taking down, you must be important. You must bring value!

Denzel Washington got a chance to explain this spiritual concept to the nation in his response to the Will Smith controversy: "There's a saying: When the devil ignores you, then you know you're doing something wrong. The devil goes, 'Oh, no, leave him alone. He's my favorite.' Conversely, when the devil comes at you, maybe it's because you're trying to do something right."

God led me through a wild series of events to get me here. The enemy intended each one of them for evil, but **God intended them for good**. Right here. Right now. Real Talk. From what's happening around the world to what's happening on this page and what's happening within you right now. Understand the love of a God who created you for this, calls you beloved, and invites you to live free. He is, as we speak, changing your name for good.

*Yours truly, Mrs. Good.*

# CHAPTER 12

# THIS CHANGES EVERYTHING

"Don't ask yourself what the world needs. Ask yourself what
makes you come alive, and then go and do that. Because what
the world needs is people who have come alive."
—Harold Whitman

God is forever calling us to higher levels. As long as we're here,
there's more to be done. Something I say often: We haven't all done the
work—and none of us have done all the work. Each decade of my life
has shown me something different, and there's always more. I'm watching Real Talk grow now from something created to help individuals
and churches to something that's changing the culture of faith and the
churches of nations. I knew there was more for me to do. I've always felt
it, but I couldn't have imagined what's happening now. The key is, God
knew, and that's why He put the unrest in me—He wanted to do all
of this and knew I'd respond. Even if it took me forever to get fully on
board.

I'm mentioning this now, though, for a reason—one that has nothing to do with me and everything to do with you. There's a connection

between the journey you've just been on (which is hopefully just the start for you) and the shift already taking place. What we've learned in *Speak the Unspeakable* is meant to help you understand your place in this world and your role in this shift. You're called to respond in a way that ignites your gifts and introduces you to the life you were meant to live.

Hopefully there's a stirring in you in the conclusion of this book that you can't ignore. Maybe it was there before and didn't have a name, maybe it's a newly ignited fire—either way, don't ignore it. The questions you're likely facing in this phase of your journey are, "How do I bring this into my life in a real way?" and for some, "How do I bring this culture into everything around me and make it the norm in my church, ministry, job, and family?" Half the battle is just asking those questions and wanting more, knowing how important this is. The other half is making a plan to step off this page and into a process.

Take a moment now in prayer and spend some time when you step away from this book to come to grips with the areas in which you feel unrest. What is your more? The last 2 percent? What have you not come to terms with? What are you still keeping hidden? Perhaps you're turning a blind eye, perhaps it's so blocked you haven't turned to face it yet and would be embarrassed like I was with the priest to admit, "Oh yeah, there is a life-altering occurrence I've locked in a titanium box." Be honest and intentional with yourself. Dig deep, and then deeper still. Change shovels and break through the limestone of your soul. Whatever it is, let's go get it—out.

This is where you "stick the landing." You stick the landing by walking it out through every step, from realizing that you were made for more, accepting that you were born to battle, and excavating full confession to seeking out and serving in your eternal purpose. This isn't just the next trend or life hack. For church leaders we talk to, we tell them that this isn't a small group study you spend some time on and move on to the next theme. This isn't a momentary spiritual high and mountaintop experience you slide right down from. In Real Talk, we've put guardrails in place, and there's a reason why:

## IT'S IRRESPONSIBLE TO ASK PEOPLE TO DIG IN AND NOT HAVE A LIFELINE READY.

I have learned from talking to leaders who were part of major ministry movements in the '80s and '90s who looked back and realized where those processes fell short and left real change on the table. They said men came to the events in the millions over the years with great enthusiasm, a captive and starved audience, but they ultimately failed. People came and had a powerful encounter, and then they sent them back to their home churches with nothing. There was no depth, no follow-up, no steps to walk it out. They didn't teach them patterns to build, give them scaffolding to uphold those patterns. Perhaps most harmful of all, they gave them absolutely no understanding of how to discover and excavate lifetimes of embedded places not yet confessed, bring them up and out, churning the soil of the soul, and rewiring the ingrained thought processes. They had one adrenaline-fueled weekend where they said it all—and then nothing. And even then, did they really talk about the secrets that were really deeply there? Confession is a powerful thing, but it's not the only thing.

They leave—and then what?

When you're done with this book, then what?

It's the whole reason we created Real Talk. Among everything else, we talk about these one-off encounter-experiences and whether something is actually going to be transformative, and we walk with you step-by-step to help guide you from your mountaintop experience to mapping out your marathon. Then we go ahead and run it with you—running alongside you with reinforcements.

One thing we say in Real Talk is that you can gauge if something is going to work in someone's life by "watching their feet" to see whether they are going to walk it out. But you can't just watch and throw them in the sea to sink or swim. You must give someone the path to walk what they've learned and a fantastic GPS system, or they're not going to have the ability to sustain change.

The encounter itself is not actually life-changing—but it gives you the *opportunity* to change your life. What comes next is the *work* and the *way*, establishing patterns and personal investment that are going to turn worlds around, starting with yours but not stopping until God-sized ideas start to come into focus and you can hardly believe the vision God had for your life all along.

## YOU GET TIRED, THEN YOU GO HIGHER.

The more you get used to the process and change your understanding and expectation level of how it works, the easier it becomes to ride the waves.

Real Talk was designed to be a key to both encounter and activation. We want to have everything in place to deliver everything that's needed to break free from what's holding you down, position you to realize your purpose, and equip you to move in this freedom for the rest of your life. What we've created is meant to provide the partnership that makes that possible.

I feel it's important to mention: This is not a commercial. It's not even really a pitch. This is personal, emotional, and missional. It's the voice of a real-life companion able to say, "I get it. I lived it.

I didn't know why no one told me what I was going through, why I was going through it, and how to walk out of it and use it for good—but I won't rest now until I share what God created with everything possible."

The ongoing setup for Real Talk isn't just rolling out a six-week program to implement in churches and small groups. A six-week can opener may be more damaging than helpful if it merely pops open all your messy secrets, discomforts, and dysfunctions, without the follow through for healing. That's just a mess without the malleability of purpose.

With Real Talk, you don't have to worry about not having support because we are a permanently ensconced coaching and consulting team that stays alongside you for the long haul. Unlike the more common model of curriculum where you go through the newest "ministry model" and Bible study, then move on to the next focus, we come into a mission-oriented partner agreement that commits to one or two years with you or your ministry—because that's how long it takes to begin to make this your norm. In that one or two years, our team works with you, your church, or leadership team through live teaching and training to raise up others to have an understanding on how to hear God in this and go through Real Talk steps ongoing and ever deeper, delving into biblical tenets and topics not talked about most Sundays.

When faced with opportunities for real institutional growth and change for their members and staff, churches, businesses, organizations, and ministries often say (and understandably so), "We don't have the capacity or people in place—we don't know how to implement this, much less keep it alive, though we want the results more than anything." That's where our team comes alongside your team, until you have it *within* your team to continue.

Something we haven't talked about a lot in this book that is possibly one of the most crucial pieces of the puzzle is Real Talk for the Next Gen.

We've talked about the impact on our kids, but mostly through how they benefit from *us* doing this work and paving the way for them. That's crucial, as we've been saying for the last twelve chapters, but every time we've mentioned it, it was in terms of us learning to lead the way for our youth, talk to them, be able to hear and respond, create spaces and off-ramps where they can talk, be unafraid, feel accepted, know they're normal, understand the battle and how it's tied to their worth and purpose (this list is as long as whatever page you're on). But it's not just on you. We created a whole Real Talk highway just for them—their age group and the unique developmental, peer-associated, and risk-evaluative situations they face.

You can see the palpable passion for this generation's freedom through the eyes of our team and my right hand and lead creator of Real Talk Next Gen, Vanessa Morris: "Never before in history has there been a greater assignment on the next generation. Our kids are inundated with lies and confusion," she says referring to the facts that one in three girls and one in five boys are being abused, that addiction to porn is setting in by age eight or nine, that the neuropathways of our children are literally being rewired based on the abusive sexual images they're seeing, that one in nine children are being approached online by predators, with shame entering instantly. All of this is met with having no one to talk to about what they've encountered, and no preemptive voice explaining what they might face and what to do about it if it happens. There's been no organized approach to fight this battle kindergarten through adulthood. Until now.

> *Real Talk is how we create a shield of protection around them, show them how to speak up and empower their voice of discernment. How they can have eyes to see and ears to hear.*[92] *How we can step into the hard conversations we've vacated for far too long. Satan has been leading the narrative of their grooming. It's time to take the territory back and safeguard our kids, showing them, they're seen, loved, and*

---

92. See Matthew 13:9–16.

*valued, giving them hope and freedom by creating safe spaces for hard conversations.*

We've tailored and customized a journey for leadership, men, women, children, and teens. We even have a version called Speak Up where the curriculum is designed for secular public schools. In every personalized application, Real Talk is the secret sauce that lights up and plugs in, **activating the greatest dormant army waiting to be put back into the game.**

Like we've said, we've talked a lot about Real Talk for a reason:

## THIS IS NOT A COMMERCIAL, THIS IS A COMMISSIONING.

It's a knighting that requests and requires you rise up, stand up, speak up—but we are not sending you out from an ivory tower to bleed out on the battlefield. Real Talk is *for* you as a personal support. I'm there, we're there. Come find your village.

You also become that village to others and have the potential to heal those in your circle of influence. If not for you (and you're entirely worth it, don't let the enemy tell you different through any of his many voices), then for the world in which you're the sweet, sweet center.

You have a choice to make now as to how you will implement all of this when you turn the next page. Whatever you do, don't stop here. Don't let go of your aha moments. Don't go back into hiding. Do *not* put that backpack back on that you hung on a hook for a hot minute while you started to trust and believe some of these promises of freedom God has laid out for you. Go forward. Ask for more. Run toward the battle and reap the reward.

I know that there are tens of thousands around the world who are waiting to be your roaring crowd of support, your personal board of directors, and your safe space of complete relief and emancipation. Not the least of which is me. Like we introduced earlier—I show up for Real Talk participants online every week taking it up a notch, no limits. And let me tell you: God is moving faster than I am or than I dreamed He would, up the ranks and across the continents. This process is being picked up and implemented by mom-and-pop shops and international governments.

It, and you, have the ability to throw the world off its off-base axis (remember when we covered the difference of a one-degree change in trajectory?) and ever so slightly back on track as a place where God's people actually show up looking like *the church*—the kind of church that isn't biased toward the powerful. The kind of church who stops for the one, dines with the lonely and the outcast.

> *TELL ME AGAIN HOW YOU DON'T DESERVE THIS? YOU DO DESERVE THIS. EQUALLY, THEY DO—THE PEOPLE YOU LOVE, THE PEOPLE GOD WANTS YOU TO REACH, THE WORLD GOD SENT YOU TO SERVE IN A POWERFUL, ETERNAL, YET-TO-BE-DISCOVERED WAY.*

Dis-Cover—uncover it. Let love loose. It changes everything and keeps changing it every day. Take my word for it; I can't stop talking about it, and I won't as long as there are more ears to hear. It changed everything in my universe for the better and for good. If you walk this out, you take a position that could change the world.

As you leave this last page of this portion of your journey, I challenge you to take a moment to pause and pray. (We have a whole team of people praying for you already.)

**Ask** for these things to take root—that the hidden will come forth, soul patterns would shift, and burdens would lift, supernaturally.

**Ask** what the next step is—that God will reveal what needs to be excavated and refine your healing journey.

**Ask** where the Good Way is—*and walk in it.*

My prayer for you is that these chapters launch your next chapter and that your journey to REAL begins now.

Welcome to the Good Life.

The World is waiting.

*This is what the Lord says: "Stand at the crossroads and look…*
*ask where the good way is, and walk in it,*
*and you will find rest for your souls."*
—Jeremiah 6:16

See you in REAL TALK! Scan the QR code or visit www.realtalkcollective.tv to begin your REAL TALK journey and join the community committed to more!

# ACKNOWLEDGEMENTS

So much gratitude! Where do I begin? Only God could have created these alignments.

Chip MacGregor, your unwavering belief in me, my message, and the call on my life means everything! Ten years ago, you said yes to working with me, and somehow way back then, you saw more than I even knew was in me—that has been the greatest gift and miracle. Thank you for your yes then, and for your continued yes over the years. Your belief in me means everything.

Amy Bartlett, well how many ways can I say WOW! I am amazed and filled with awe and wonder at how God aligned my voice with your heart. Thank you! Each time you said, "No one talks like this, and no one is saying this," was truly a balm to my soul and an accelerator. Your immediate excitement and yes was a gift beyond measure. And I love how you said, "Each time you speak you say something different"; it was the truth as the messaging was downloading real time, fast and furious! Such gratitude to you for your speed and gifting to interpret me and all my ways. Your divine talent landed the ship and helped it all come out powerful and REAL!

Christine Whitaker, what a rare gem you are! In a world that grows faster and faster, filled with noise and distractions, your voice and spirit cuts through and you are a treasured calm in the storm. You have powerful vision, discernment, what you are seeing is good... and yes, you should DO IT ALL! You are building something powerful, and I am so grateful to be in your house! I feel tremendously fortunate and blessed. Thank you, Whitaker family!

Vanessa Morris, my right hand, and girl wonder! There would be no me without you. The last twelve years have been wild and crazy— but having you alongside made each moment safe and good! You are brilliant in ALL ways, and I wouldn't want to lead and build this wild thing with anyone else! Thank you for all you are and your vast brilliance in creating what has never existed before! To infinity and beyond! As we know it will always involve a rocket ship!

And to the entire REAL TALK team that first said yes—Diana Walston, Alan Wilkette, and Chip McCall. So much fun doing this together—thank you!

My amazing PIT Crew—you are priceless.

Manna, thank you for making it happen, and Beth, Dawn, Melissa, Deb, Cathy, Elaine, and Gloria...thank you for every day!

And to you Jill, Netty, and Bill for your extra layer of secret sauce! What a POWERFUL crew!

My Board of Directors at The Foundation United, my Pretorian guard; "Oh, how I love you!" Lynne Jubilee, Fred Feller, Ruth LeFebvre, and Jeff Rech, thank you for believing in me, my mission and calling, and covering me well so I can build and soar as God leads.

And to Mr. Good and my kiddos—thank you for enduring all! It is a journey.

So much love and gratitude.

xo E